D0110918

Smoking Accessories

A Collector's Guide

Sarah Yates

Special Consultant:
Jacques Cole

MILLER'S SMOKING ACCESSORIES: A COLLECTOR'S GUIDE
by Sarah Yates
Special Consultant: Jacques Cole

First published in Great Britain in 2000 by Miller's, a division of
Mitchell Beazley, imprints of Octopus Publishing Group Ltd,
2–4 Heron Quays, London E14 4JP

Miller's is a registered trademark of Octopus Publishing Group Ltd

Commissioning Editor **Anna Sanderson**
Executive Art Editor **Vivienne Brar**
Editor **Selina Mumford**
Designer **Louise Griffiths**
Picture Research **Jenny Faithfull**
Production **Jessame Emms**
Indexer **Sue Farr**
Proofreader **Laura Hicks**
Specially commissioned photography by **A J Photographics &**
    Steve Tanner
Jacket photograph by **Steve Tanner**

ISBN 1 84000 187 9
A CIP record for this book is available from the British Library
Set in Bembo, Frutiger and Shannon
Colour reproduction by HK Scanner Arts INT'L Ltd.
Produced by Toppan Printing Co., (HK) Ltd
Printed and bound in China

Jacket illustrations, front clockwise from top: meerschaum pipe,
c.1900, £80–100/$130–160; silver snuff box, 1844,
£600–800/$960–1,280; vesta case, 19thC, £100–150/$160–240;
cigarette case, 1898, £300–400/$480–640. Back: vesta case, 1886,
£2,800–3,000/$4,500–4,800

Smoking Accessories

A Collector's Guide

contents

Introduction

When Christopher Columbus landed on Hispaniola (as it was first called) in 1492, he was probably welcomed by natives offering tobacco leaves. He did not know what the leaves were until two of his companions, Luis de Torres and Rodrigo de Jerez, came across Cuban natives on the island rolling these leaves, lighting them, and inhaling the smoke. Tobacco took some time to come across the Atlantic to England, but it became popular in the latter half of the 16thC. However, reports of pipe-smoking sailors came from northern English and Scottish ports around 1525.

Clay was the first material used in Europe for pipemaking. The pipes were modelled on Native American styles, and were quite small, owing to the original high price of tobacco. By 1600 many potters had taken up clay pipemaking, and in England the first centres were around the main ports, such as Hull and Whitehaven. In London and Bristol there were several hundred pipemakers, who supplied not only England but also the American colonies.

In 1616 the first major shipment of tobacco leaf arrived in England from Virginia and it is recorded that in 1620 40,000lb of tobacco were imported into the country. James I attacked tobacco in his "Counterblaste" (1604), but this did not stop him granting a charter to the pipemakers of Westminster. It did, however, encourage William Barentz, a dissenter, to take his pipemaking skills to The Netherlands, where he joined the Dutch clay pipe industry in Gouda.

As far as collectors of smoking wares are concerned, this period is quite interesting; clay pipes were cheap, but fragile, so they broke easily, although some can be found intact.

Originally there were no ideas about collecting, but models specially made for trade guilds, professions, even inns, and other subjects were probably kept. At the time clay pipes were mainly made in England, Scotland, The Netherlands, Belgium, and northern France. There were early smokers' accessories, although few are preserved, apart from tobacco jars and a scattering of lead boxes.

In the 18thC, snuff taking became fashionable in England, following a Continental trend and also after the British Fleet captured a huge amount of snuff from Spanish ships. This period is therefore rich in snuff-boxes of all shapes and sizes, in materials ranging from ordinary wood (such as boxwood) to elaborate luxury containers made of pewter, silver, or gold, and embellished with enamel and precious stones. They were often exchanged as presents, or given as rewards by monarchs or other potentates for services rendered. At the time, a number of important snuff-box collections began to take shape.

The golden age of smoking was undoubtedly the 19thC. Pipes were produced in a variety of materials, such as meerschaum and ceramic, that had already been used in the latter part of the 18thC, but by the 1800s a rich range of artistic models had been made, and today these items are often the basis of valuable collections. Vienna was the main centre of meerschaum carving, and some of the pipes produced there are of exquisite detail. Hungary, Germany, France, and Sweden also made very fine meerschaum models. A very special type of porcelain pipe, highly decorated with a variety of subjects, including military, was made in Germany and Austria.

Clay pipes enjoyed a revival, when not only did the quality improve, but also the range of figural pipes manufactured caught the imagination of smokers. France led the way, and a number of subjects which were popular at the time, including politicians, generals, historical figures, and living personalities, are now sought after by collectors. Of course, The Netherlands and Britain also produced a very similar type of pipe, as did Belgium, Italy, and Spain; clay pipes were also made in the USA. From the 1850s, the use of briar wood in pipemaking added another dimension to the possibilities of collecting. Many finely carved pieces from the second half of the 19thC still exist.

Cigars became popular at the beginning of the 19thC, the habit having been picked up in Spain by soldiers from Britain, France, and other nations. At the time of the Crimean War, soldiers discovered the cigarette, and these "new" smoking habits also crossed the Atlantic to the USA and Canada.

All these developments generated a wealth of accessories: pipe cases, cigar and cigarette cases and boxes in leather, silver, gold, and other materials; tobacco pouches and jars, plus other wares such as tampers, cigar cutters, and vesta cases. From the first decade of the 20thC, the modern lighter joined the old tinder boxes, and other early lighting implements, to enhance further the vast range of collectables. This book has selected some of the best examples of collectable articles, but there is only room to scratch the surface. Not only are all sorts of items found in Europe and North America, but also ethnic pieces from the Middle East, India, China, Japan, all parts of Africa, and Central and South America are of great interest. Modern articles have joined the ranks of possibilities for collectors, and even current manufacturers produce "limited editions" to encourage collecting.

On these pages the accessories shown are (*opposite*) a Dutch tortoiseshell cigar case, c.1790–1800, **£150–200/$240–320**; (*above*) an Alfred Dunhill Quaint Shape Bruyere pipe, 1920s, **£800–1,200/$1,280–1,900**; (*below*) a silver, gilt-lined, enamelled cigarette case, London, 1937, **£300–400/$480–640**.

Jacques Coles

Early smoking wares

When tobacco was introduced into Europe in the 16thC by traders and explorers, it was initially popular mainly for its supposed medicinal powers. However, despite the efforts of such rulers as James I of England to discourage pipe-smoking, the fashion spread, so that by 1614 there were allegedly over 7,000 tobacco sellers in London. Tobacco was usually sold and stored at home in large jars – made of lead, pewter, pottery, and, in the 18thC, porcelain – from which the smoker refilled a small tobacco box to carry a daily supply. The famous smoker Sir Walter Raleigh is said to have had a silver pipe, but most people could only afford clay ones; early 17thC examples had very small bowls, reflecting the high cost of tobacco. Before the invention of friction matches in the early 19thC, the smoker had to rely on a tinder box to create a flame to light his or her pipe.

▼ **Staffordshire pottery pipe**

During the late 18thC and early 19thC, well-known potteries in Staffordshire, including Thomas Whieldon and the Pratt family of Fenton, produced some unusual pipes in lead-glazed earthenware. Made as a purely decorative piece, this type of novelty pipe is known as a "heart in the hand": the bowl of the pipe is modelled as a female head, and held in a hand on the palm of which is a red heart; the precise significance of the design is not known.

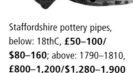

Staffordshire pottery pipes, below: 18thC, **£50–100/ $80–160**; above: 1790–1810, **£800–1,200/$1,280–1,900**

▲ **Staffordshire pottery pipe**

Like "heart in the hand" pipes, "puzzle" pipes were not designed to be smoked. This type of pipe was made by coiling a single, long tube of unfired clay, with a bowl at one end and a mouthpiece at the other. The pipe was then decorated in a distinctive palette of blue, orange, green, yellow, and purple, sometimes in patterns imitating snake markings. Such pipes are particularly rare in good condition today, and consequently can fetch high prices.

▼ Tobacco jars

Tobacco jars were produced from the mid 17thC and had tightly fitting lids and, inside, a flat, lead disc (known as a presser) to keep the tobacco fresh. Lead – a poor heat conductor – was the favourite material in England, owing to the English preference for moist, cool tobacco. Jars are often decorated with sporting or hunting scenes; many were painted in bright colours, but the paint has usually flaked off. Pewter jars, some with finely detailed, naturalistic scenes or stylized patterns, were modelled on contemporary silver shapes. Pottery jars were widely produced in the 19thC.

Tobacco jars, 18th and 19thC, **£40–60/ $65–95 each**; from left to right: pottery, pewter, lead

Snuff bottle, 18th or 19thC, **£800–1,200/ $1,280–1,900**

◀ Aquamarine-glass snuff bottle

Snuff was introduced into China by Europeans in the mid 17thC. In China bottles rather than boxes were the preferred means of storage. Chinese snuff bottles, as in the West, were often made from luxurious materials, such as porcelain, jade, rock crystal, and hardstones, and presented as gifts. The rounded, rectangular design of this glass bottle, finely carved with ornament in the style of ancient Chinese bronzes, is fairly unusual, as most were elliptical in shape. Like many high-quality pieces, it has a stopper made of a more expensive material, in this case rose quartz.

Small tinder boxes

A box contained a flint and steel, and a daily supply of tinder. The finest quality boxes were fashioned from silver, brass, pewter, or ivory, and sometimes embellished with the monogram or armorials of the owner. Many are similar to later snuff boxes, but some have a steel set on the box.

▼ Blue-glass snuff bottle

This globular, blue-glass snuff bottle, with a matching stopper, is splashed with gold; other Chinese glass snuff bottles were carved or painted with enamels, or, particularly in the 19thC, painted inside. A small spoon would have been attached to the inside of the lid for extracting the snuff. Dating Chinese snuff bottles is difficult, as there are very few precisely dated examples, though some are marked with the reign period names of the emperors.

Glass snuff bottle, 18th or 19thC, **£300–500/$480–800**

Tobacco boxes pre 1820

Tobacco was originally stored at home in large tobacco jars, but from the 17thC small tobacco boxes were introduced. These were generally shallow, oblong, and fitted with a hinged lid to keep the tobacco fresh. As they were intended to be portable, most tobacco boxes were made from lightweight, sheet brass and copper, but pewter, steel, and silver were other popular materials. Boxes engraved with often humorous scenes of smoking, drinking, country sports, and domestic life were a speciality of Dutch makers from the early 17thC – The Netherlands was one of the biggest traders in tobacco and tobacco-related products – although many boxes were manufactured in Germany and England, where pipe-smoking remained popular even after the craze for snuff began in the 18thC.

◄ **English tortoiseshell tobacco box**
Most tobacco boxes were made entirely of metal, so a tortoiseshell piece is particularly scarce and valuable. The hinged lid of the box is fashioned from a single small shell from a turtle or tortoise – this would have been collected as a rare specimen, and highly prized – and is mounted in a metal rim to protect it from damage. Unusually, this oval box contains a tobacco tamper for pressing down burning tobacco in a pipe.

Tortoiseshell tobacco box, **£1,100–1,300/ $1,750–2,000**

▼ **Dutch tobacco box**
This box has a plain border around the edge of the lid, and is engraved with a panorama of Delft in the manner of Dutch landscape paintings of the time; other common subjects on Dutch boxes include scenes of tavern life, hunting, bear-baiting, ships, and sailors. Many copies of boxes of this type were made in the 1920s and 1930s, and it can be difficult to distinguish them from originals; the smoothed corners and traces of oxidization on the lid of this box are, however, good indications of age.

Dutch brass tobacco box, c.1720–50, **£400–500/ $640–800**

Dutch tobacco box, c.1720–50,
£400–450/$640–720

Identification
- English: plainer than Continental boxes; silver boxes often engraved only with armorials
- Dutch: usually oblong and made in brass or copper; floral scroll or moulded ropework borders common
- German: oblong with curved ends; most signed with decorator's or maker's name or initials

▲ Dutch tobacco box
Dutch and German boxes were often decorated on both lid and base – this brass box is engraved with a portrait of the Prince of Orange on the lid, and his consort on the underside, with a coat of arms, and an inscription relating to the Dutch royal House of Orange. Similar boxes, engraved with patriotic verses, and portraits of Lord Nelson, or the Duke of Wellington, were produced in England in the 19thC. Engraved scenes on Dutch boxes are rarely signed, which makes them difficult to date.

▼ German tobacco box
Iserlohn in western Germany, where this brass box was produced, was a renowned centre for the manufacture of high-quality copper and brass tobacco boxes during the second half of the 18thC, and boxes made there were exported throughout Europe. Its oblong form, rounded corners, and finely detailed, embossed decoration are typical of 18thC German boxes. The embossed scene and inscription on the lid commemorate the military victories of Frederick the Great, King of Prussia. Battle scenes with round medallion portraits at either end are also found on German boxes of this period.

German tobacco box, c.1720–50,
£400–450/$640–720

Dutch tobacco box, c.1730,
£550–600/$880–960

▲ Dutch tobacco box
This unusual, and rare, circular, Dutch box is fitted with a combination lock – the brass pointers on the lid must be turned to the correct setting before the box will open. Such novelty features were widely used on tobacco and, later, snuff boxes, since tobacco was an expensive commodity before the 19thC. The decorative, engraved tulips around the lid indicate the box's Dutch origin.

Early snuff boxes

The craze for snuff began at the royal court of France in the 16thC, and by the end of the 17thC snuff-taking was considered the height of elegance for both men and women. The English preferred pipe-smoking, but the fashion for snuff spread after 50,000kg (50 tons) of the finest Havana snuff was captured from the Spanish by the English naval fleet at Vigo Bay in 1702. Snuff was originally made by grating tightly rolled tobacco leaves, but from the early 18thC ready-ground snuff was available. Generally oval, square, or rectangular, snuff boxes were made in a huge range of styles and materials, from wood and horn for the simplest, to hardstone, enamel, silver, and gold for the most luxurious.

▼ **English, double-ended, silver snuff box**
This rare, early, London-made snuff box has an unusual, waisted form, and two compartments for different varieties of snuff. The simple mouldings, and restrained decoration of an engraved coat of arms, are typical of English silver of the first half of the 18thC. It is always important to check that the engraving is contemporary with the piece: a coat of arms was often "erased", and a new one re-engraved, when an item changed ownership; this can be identified by a thinness in the metal around the engraving.

English silver snuff box, 1741,
£600–800/$960–1,280

Scottish silver snuff box, maker's mark RH, Edinburgh, 1818,
£200–300/$320–480

◀ **Scottish silver snuff box**
The Scots were renowned for their habit of snuff-taking throughout the 19thC, when it had gone out of fashion elsewhere in Europe. While mulls (see p. 14) were widely used as snuff containers, silver boxes were also produced in the major cities, such as Edinburgh, where this box was made. They are generally plainer than contemporary English pieces; the lid of this gilt-lined piece is engraved with a simple crest and motto.

Snuff spoons

To avoid losing precious snuff, many boxes were supplied with matching spoons for ease of handling. It is very rare to find a box with its original spoon, since this was often mislaid, but some single spoons can be found today. Made in all flatware (cutlery) patterns, they can be identified by their small sizes (5–6cm/2–2½in long).

Tortoiseshell snuff box, early 18thC, **£150–200/$240–320**

▼ English silver-gilt snuff box

During the late 18thC the introduction of mechanical techniques of rolling and die-stamping sheet silver meant that silver snuff boxes could be produced in quantity, and sold at lower prices, which made them available to a wider section of society. Most boxes of this type were mass-produced in Birmingham, but this piece was made in London. It is particularly desirable as the detail on the die-stamped lid is still sharp, and scenes of hunting dogs are among the most popular with collectors.

Silver-gilt snuff box, London, 1819, **£400–600/$640–960**

▲ Tortoiseshell snuff box

Tortoiseshell was a favourite material for snuff boxes, as it had excellent insulating properties, and kept the snuff in good condition. It was widely used for small, decorative items in England after it was introduced in the late 17thC by Jean Obrisset (c.1666–c.1728), son of a French ivory carver, who specialized in tortoiseshell medallion portraits of English royalty. This box in the form of a book has pierced and chased silver mounts and hinges.

German snuff box, Johann Christian Neuber, Dresden, 1775, **£2,500–3,000/$4,000–4,800**

▲ German, hardstone, porcelain-and-gold snuff box

J.C. Neuber (1736–1808) was the leading maker of luxurious, gold-and-hardstone boxes at the Dresden court of Frederick Augustus II, Elector of Saxony, during the early 18thC. This piece is set with small, shaped, hardstone panels in a lattice pattern, though many of Neuber's circular, oval, or octagonal boxes have radiating patterns.

Ivory snuff box, late 17th/early
18thC, **£250–300/$400–480**

▲ **French ivory snuff box**
The reign of Louis XIV
(1643–1715) was among
the most notable for ivory
carvings in France, especially
in Dieppe, where this box was
probably made. The relatively
large size of this box (9cm/
3½in long) suggests that it
may have been a table snuff
box for communal use. Ivory
boxes were often presented as
diplomatic gifts by the French
court, and the hinged lid of
this box, with silver mounts,
is elaborately carved with a
profile of Louis XIV – who
actually disliked snuff –
between masks and foliage.

Bone snuff box, c.1790,
£120–150/$190–240

▲ **Bone snuff box**
To help pass the time, French
prisoners held in England
during the Napoleonic Wars
(1790s–1815) carved a variety
of small objects such as boxes,
crucifixes, buttons, combs, and
dominoes from animal bones
saved from their meals. Such
items were often sold to the
local population at markets
held in the prison yards.
The prisoners also made
marquetry items out of straw
from their beds. Such pieces
are often popular with
collectors of militaria today.

Horn snuff mull, late 18th/early
19thC, **£100–150/$160–240**

▲ **Scottish horn snuff mull**
Mulls were a type of snuff
container peculiar to Scotland,
and were made from polished
ram, ox, or goat horn (or
sometimes ivory, ebony,
or lignum vitae), with applied
silver or silver-gilt mounts;
the hinged cover was often
set with rock crystal or Scottish
semi-precious stones. The
elaborately coiled end of this
mull was created by heating
or boiling the horn until it was
soft and flexible, then curling
it around a stick. Sometimes
chained implements are
attached to the mull, such
as rakes and hammers to
break up caked snuff, and
a preserved hare's foot
to remove snuff from
the moustache.

Enamelled snuff
box, c.1765,
£200–250/$320–400

▲ Birmingham enamelled snuff box

During the late 18thC
and early 19thC, many
decorative, enamel-on-
copper, English snuff
boxes were mass-produced in
Birmingham and Staffordshire.
The technique of fusing flint
glass to copper under heat,
to produce a white, vitreous
surface – which could then be
overpainted in polychrome
enamels – was introduced into
England from France during
the 17thC. Like this example,
Birmingham snuff and patch
boxes were frequently transfer-
printed, in vivid colours, with
landscapes or genre scenes.
They were often sold as
mementos at fashionable
resorts.

Enamelled snuff box, 1780,
£100–150/$160–240

▲ South Staffordshire enamelled snuff box

The enamelled lid features
green sprigs and flower
posies, imitating the style of
decoration on contemporary
European porcelain. Like most
English enamel-on-copper
boxes, it is set in gilt-metal
mounts, but there is some
slight damage to this piece
which will reduce the value:
the delicate enamel is easily
chipped, and the mounts
sometimes dented. Square
and oblong shapes are
the most common for
enamelled boxes, but
some novelty designs,
such as miniature musical
instruments,' are also found
on the market today.

▼ Lacquered snuff box

Wooden boxes are the most
common type of snuff box,
and were made in a multitude
of designs. Often apprentices
carved novelty shapes
connected with their professions
such as shoes and boats,
from small, leftover pieces of
wood. Decorative finishes were
equally varied, and included
transfer-printed topographical
scenes or painted sporting
scenes. This box would be
particularly valuable owing
to the collecting interest in
cricketing memorabilia.

Lacquered wooden snuff box,
18thC, **£200–300/$320–480**

Late snuff boxes

Snuff-taking reached its height of popularity in the late 18thC and early 19thC: in France, Napoleon I, for example, reputedly used 3.2kg (7lb) a month, while in England George IV gave snuff boxes worth £8,000 to visiting diplomats and dignitaries at his coronation in 1820. Also in England in the 19thC, silver snuff boxes became available to a wider market as they were mass-produced in Birmingham by the new mechanical techniques of die-stamping and rolling sheet silver. However, the vast majority of boxes in this period were made of wood, either carved, painted, or transfer-printed. New novelty shapes, such as shoes, barrels, and hats, were produced, in addition to the simple, rectangular, box form.

▼ **English silver snuff box**
Battle scenes were a favoured subject of decoration for many snuff boxes, since snuff taking was a particularly masculine habit. The high relief, and fine detailing, of the soldiers and flags on the lid of this box suggest that it was cast in silver rather than die-stamped. Cast pieces, which are particularly valuable today, can also be identified by their heavier weight, as die-stamped pieces were made from thin-gauge sheet silver.

Silver snuff box, Thomas Shaw, Birmingham, 1826,
£700–1,000/ $1,120– 1,600

▲ **English silver snuff box**
This box is known as a "castle-top": one depicting a famous building or landmark in England. The most successful exponent of this type of decoration was the silversmith Nathaniel Mills – his works are likely to fetch at least twice as much as this piece, by a lesser-known maker. Boxes depicting identifiable buildings outside the major cities are more sought after than those showing well-known landmarks.

Silver snuff box showing Windsor Castle, England, Edward Smith, Birmingham, 1844,
£600–800/ $960–1,280

- Pieces with cast or enamelled decoration, or hunting, battle, or castle-top scenes, are desirable
- Always check hinges and mounts for denting and splitting
- Lids should be tight-fitting and close properly
- Engraved or bright-cut decoration should be well-defined and sharp
- Well-known 19thC makers include Alexander Strachan and Nathaniel Mills

▼ English silver snuff box

Racehorses were a popular theme of decoration for smoking accessories: this snuff box shows a horse – probably named "Alarm", as indicated by the inscription – and jockey on the lid, while the base is engraved with two horses in a field. The all-over pattern of exuberant scrolls, shells, and leaves is typical of Victorian engraving or flat-chasing. During the 19thC, much earlier plain silver was embellished with flat-chasing in this style. On such pieces, the chasing will be superimposed over the hallmarks; pieces engraved or chased at the time of manufacture were hallmarked after they were decorated.

Silver snuff box, maker's mark E.E., London, 1846, **£300–400/$480–640**

▼ English silver snuff dispenser

This unusual snuff dispenser in the form of a plain powder flask – possibly made for a military officer – is relatively late in date. The fashion for snuff declined after the invention of the friction match in 1826 made cigar smoking more popular, but snuff mulls and containers, for British Army regiments, were made well into the Edwardian era. This one has a stopper at one end, and a ring for suspending it from a chain at the other, similar to a vesta case – in fact, many snuff box makers turned to the manufacture of vesta cases in the late 19thC.

Silver snuff dispenser, maker's mark EHS, retailed by Thornhills, London, 1875, **£600–800/ $960–1,280**

▼ Tortoiseshell snuff box

Tortoiseshell was a popular material for snuff boxes, since it could be easily moulded and welded into various shapes, and was less expensive than gold or silver. This elegant piece is inset with an enamel miniature portrait of a military officer, and its circular form, and simple metal banding decoration, are characteristic of the restrained style of many early 19thC boxes.

Tortoiseshell snuff box, early 19thC, **£150–200/$240–320**

Papier-mâché snuff box, 19thC, **£50–60/$80–95**

Shell snuff boxes, mid 19thC, **£40–50/$65–80 each**

▲ Papier-mâché snuff box

During the 19thC, papier-mâché was widely used for making inexpensive snuff boxes, as it was economical to produce, it could be shaped into any form, and, most importantly, it insulated the snuff against heat, cold, and damp. Like this piece, decorated with a Madonna and Child in the style of Raphael, the lids were often painted in oils, although japanning (imitation lacquer), mother-of-pearl inlay, and pasted and varnished prints were also popular. Good condition is important, as many 19thC papier-mâché pieces are prone to cracking and flaking.

Coquilla-nut snuff box, mid 19thC, **£140–170/$220–270**

▲ Coquilla-nut snuff box

The coquilla, a type of nut grown in swamps on the eastern coast of South America, was introduced into Europe during the mid 16thC, and was widely used for small carved objects in countries such as Italy, France, and England until the late 19thC. This piece is carved with heads and figures, but animals, boats, shells, and Biblical scenes were other, common, decorative motifs.

▲ Shell snuff boxes

Shells, often collected for their curiosity value during the Victorian period, were ideal for transforming into snuff boxes, since metal mounts could simply be applied at the blunt end of the hinged shell to create a lid and base. A variety of shells were used – those shown here are cockle (*left*), cowrie (*bottom*), and mussel (*top*) – and mounts were made of silver, silver-gilt, pewter, brass, or pinchbeck, according to the means and taste of the owner. Such pieces are more accessible to the collector today than expensive chased and enamelled boxes, but it is important to check that the shell is not chipped, and that the mounts, often made of thin metal, are not dented.

Shoes
Shoes were a particularly popular form for novelty snuff boxes and, later, vesta cases; they were a symbol of marriage, and so often presented as a gift or love token. Most shoe-shaped boxes were made in inexpensive materials such as papier-mâché or wood.

Enamelled silver snuff box, 19thC,
£400–600/ $640–960

▲ **French, enamelled, silver snuff box**
Like the rectangular enamelled box also shown (see *right*), this piece is a fine-quality imitation of 18thC fashions: it is inset with an enamelled miniature, in the style of the French Rococo painter Antoine Watteau, and its oval shape, and border of engine-turning, overlaid with translucent, *guilloché* enamel, copy the form and decoration of earlier French snuff boxes. The applied, cast thumbpiece is also an indication of fine craftsmanship, although the best examples are often chased with shells, scrolls, and flowers.

Enamelled silver snuff box, late 19thC,
£300–400/$480–640

▲ **Continental European enamelled silver snuff box**
This elegant enamelled silver box is typical of the Classical style revived in the late 19thC, as is shown by its rectangular form, fine *guilloché* border, muted palette, and mytho-logical painting in an oval frame. The subtle colours and fine detail indicate that the enamelling is contemporary with the box: modern, reproduction enamels can be identified by coarse brushwork and harsh colours. Enamelled pieces are particularly sought after among collectors today.

Mauchlineware snuff box, c.1810,
£200–300/$320–480

▲ **Mauchlineware snuff box**
Mauchlineware souvenirs, such as snuff boxes and cigar cases, were produced in Scotland, mainly for tourists, during the 19thC. Portraits of the Scottish poet Robert Burns (1759–96) and verses of his poetry were, as seen on this box made from elm root, two of the favourite decorative themes, but landscapes, sporting scenes, armorials, and tartan patterns were also common.

Bryant & May

Surprisingly, the first friction matches were invented as late as 1826 by John Walker. As he did not patent his invention – sold as "Friction Lights" – matchmaking factories multiplied rapidly throughout Europe. From the 1830s, deadly white phosphorus – causing "phossy jaw" – was added to the matches, but this was replaced by harmless red phosphoros in the safety match invented in 1855 by the Swedish engineer Johan Edvard Lundstrom. In the same year he sold the British patent rights to William Bryant and Francis May, and by 1862 they were producing nearly two million matches per week. Bryant & May is now part of Swedish Match, but its products are so well known that its Swan Vestas are the only match brand to be asked for by name.

▶ **Vesta tin**
Early matches were highly combustible, and so for safety reasons were often sold and stored in tin boxes. With the advent of the safety match, however, tins became an important means of advertising for the match manufacturer. From 1877, Bryant & May held the patent for the use of offset lithography – a method that enabled a coloured design to be printed directly onto the tin – and manufactured a wide variety of tins for its own products and those of other companies. This tin for vestas (wax matches) features a somewhat sinister design of men being beheaded.

Vesta tin, c.1880,
£30–40/$50–65

▼ **Souvenir match tin**
Throughout the late 19thC and the 20thC, matchboxes and tins were produced to commemorate various international exhibitions, such as the 1851 Great Exhibition at Crystal Palace, and the 1924/25 British Empire Exhibition, as well as royal weddings, coronations, and jubilees. This tin, containing "Bryant & May's Celebrated Wax Vestas", commemorates the Chicago World Fair of 1893, with a detailed view of the fair on both lid and base.

Souvenir match tin, 1893,
£90–£100/$145–160

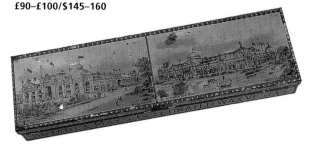

Matchbox of "Flaming Fusees"

Fusee matches, also known as "Vesuvians" or "Flamers", were developed in the mid 19thC for lighting a pipe or cigar out of doors; they have very large heads, coated with a mixture of charcoal, sawdust, bark, and phosphorus, designed to burn for up to 20 seconds in even the fiercest wind. However, the unsupported, heavy match head often fell off the stem while still alight, setting fire to clothes and furnishings, so a method of "braiding" – reinforcing the heads with cotton thread or wire – was developed. This early box has a typically simple design, with the original striking surface on the side.

"Flaming Fusees", c.1865, **£50–60/ $80–95**

Matchbox of "Braided Cigar Lights"

"Braided Cigar Lights' were similar to fusee matches, though cigar tips and caps were aimed specifically at the cigar smoker. Cigar tips comprised a small wooden stick, with an inflammable head, that was inserted into the end of the cigar, and the head struck on the side of the box; cigar caps – small paper cones with inflammable tips – worked in a similar fashion. Like the box of "Flaming Fusees", this box complete with its contents will be more valuable than an empty box of the same date.

"Braided Cigar Lights", 1865, **£60–70/$95–110**

Matchbox labels

single: paper label pasted on top or bottom of the sliding tray; **all-round paper sleeve:** if the paper is cut in two it will render the label worthless; **skillet:** cardboard outer cover on which the design is directly printed; **pill box:** circular paper label pasted to the top of cylindrical boxes; **banderole:** paper label around a circular matchbox

"Tiger" matches

"Tiger" matches were one of only several Bryant & May match brands. While many labels were often reprinted as stocks ran low, some have been printed as fakes: check for sharp lines and bright colours, and paper that has not faded; many Victorian labels will fade when exposed to sunlight, so must be carefully stored.

"Tiger" matches, 1880, **£30–40/$50–65**

Vesta cases

The vesta case is a small box used for carrying wax vesta matches, which were first produced in the 1840s. These matches, made from thick cotton threads dipped in paraffin wax, with phosphorus heads that ignited when rubbed, were initially sold in cardboard boxes with sandpaper or emery paper attached for striking; as these easily caught fire, they needed to be kept in boxes of less combustible materials. There are three main types of vesta case: wall-mounted, freestanding for a desk or table, and pocket size. The last type, most widely collected today, became popular from the mid 19thC, after the invention of the safety match in 1855 enabled matches to be carried on the person. Called matchsafes in the USA, they are generally 3.75–7.5cm (1½–3in) long, with sprung, hinged lids; a serrated edge forms a striker for lighting the match.

▼ **Silver vesta case in the shape of a bear**

Animal-shaped cases were particularly popular during the late 19thC, and remain so with collectors today; they include dogs, mice, owls, turtles, elephants, frogs, rats, sheep, and snakes, as well as bears. The excellent condition, fine detailing, and appealing subject of this case make it particularly sought after by collectors; beware of similar, modern reproductions, on which features such as the hair are less well-defined, and which have strikers with shallow rather than sharp grooves.

Bear-shaped silver vesta case, c.1880, **£400–600/ $640–960**

▶ **Silver vesta case in form of a lock**

This English vesta case is typical of the Victorian fashion for making match cases with ingenious or trick opening devices; other examples are sometimes painted with a message saying "Help Yourself", but it is impossible to open the case without knowing a certain combination. The hallmarks are clearly visible on this piece, and they should always be present on solid silver vesta cases made in England; beware of cases on which the marks have been worn through excessive handling, as this will reduce value.

Silver "lock" vesta case, Birmingham, 1882, **£250–300/ $400–480**

Enamelled decoration
Enamelled vesta cases
are particularly sought
after by collectors today,
and are more expensive
than plain, engraved, or
engine-turned cases. Chips
or dents in enamel are
very difficult to repair,
so only buy pieces in
good condition. Genuine
enamel produces a dull
sound when tapped:
modern "plastic" enamel
will produce a sharp,
metallic sound.

Enamelled silver vesta case,
by George Unite, 1885,
£500–600/$800–960

▲ **Enamelled silver
vesta case**
During the late 19thC
smoking was widespread
in the leisured classes, and,
correspondingly, designs
on silver cases were often
inspired by shooting, hunting,
and other gentlemanly
outdoor sports. Cases with
high-quality, enamelled
hunting scenes are especially
sought after today. The fine
detailing and sharp colours
of the enamelling on this solid
silver English case indicate
that the decoration is
contemporary with the case;
modern "plastic" enamelling
is characterized by awkward,
clumsy designs, and muddy
colours. Genuine enamels
are also often covered with
a pattern of tiny scratches,
as a result of rubbing against
coins and watches.

Enamelled silver vesta case, by
Sampson Mordan & Co., 1886,
£2,800–3,000/$4,500–4,800

▲ **Enamelled silver
vesta case**
This exceptionally rare vesta
case, in the shape of a sentry
box, is one of a set of possibly
12 with enamelled designs.
showing guards of different
British Army regiments,
produced by Sampson
Mordan & Co. from 1886
onwards. This case illustrates
a soldier in the Household
Brigade; other examples show
the 17th Lancers, the Black
Watch, and the Life Guards.
Sampson Mordan & Co. was a
prolific London manufacturer
of very fine quality enamelled
vesta cases and other small
silverware, and its work is
particularly sought after today.

▼ **Silver vesta case**
Many vesta cases were made
in the form of different
containers, such as barrels and
suitcases; this Birmingham-
made piece is modelled
as a water bottle in a basket.
The ring and chain would
enable the smoker to attach
the case to a watch chain;
it is important to check that
all the links in the chain are
in good condition.

Silver vesta case, 1888,
£400–600/$640–960

Silver vesta case

Sampson Mordan & Co. was one of the leading manufacturers of fine silver vesta cases, and this owl case will be more valuable than one of similar date by another maker. The rough surface of the owl's feathers was probably used as the striking surface; this area, as well as the hinges on the owl's head, which forms the lid, and the glass eyes, should be checked carefully for damage, as this will reduce the value.

Silver vesta case, Sampson Mordan & Co., London, 1895, **£600–800/$960–1,280**

Brass vesta case

The subject of this English enamelled and plated brass case is Ally Sloper, a character in an early British popular comic paper called *Ally Sloper's Half Holiday* (1884–1923); the name referred to an unemployed man who would "slope off" to avoid paying the rent collector. The character is always shown, as here, wearing a battered top hat, and was also frequently depicted on clay pipes. As with many unusual or figural designs for cases, this one was patented by Frederick W. Tomkinson, a die-sinker in Birmingham. Although the paint around the face is scratched and chipped, this novelty design is still highly collectable.

"Ally Sloper", Frederick W. Tomkinson, 1888, **£300–400/$480–640**

Brass vesta case

As was William Gladstone (*see right*), under whom he served as a cabinet minister, Joseph Chamberlain was a popular subject for late Victorian brass vesta cases. He was Mayor of Birmingham from 1873 to 1876; his second son was Neville Chamberlain. This design was registered by Jenkin W. Evans, a die-sinker, stamper, and piercer in Birmingham in 1888. Many brass cases were often plated with a thin layer of nickel or silver to simulate solid silver, but, as on this case, it has often been removed by gradual wear or modern cleaning abrasives, which will reduce its value.

"Joseph Chamberlain", Jenkin W. Evans, c.1888, **£150–200/$240–320**

▼ Brass vesta case

Inexpensive brass cases in a great variety of novelty designs – such as animals, hearts, books, hats, crowns, insects, and portrait heads, such as this bust of William Ewart Gladstone – were produced in vast quantities in the late 19thC, particularly in Birmingham. Such cases are much less expensive and more common than silver or gold pieces on the market today. Other subjects of portrait cases include both contemporary and historical figures, such as Christopher Columbus and Richard the Lionheart. In the USA, figural vesta cases of presidents such as Grover Cleveland, William McKinley, and Ulysses S. Grant were often given away as political campaign mementos.

"William Gladstone", 1880s,
£120–150/$190–240

▼ Japanese vesta case

Japanese art enjoyed great popularity in Europe and the USA during the 1890s and early 1900s, inspiring a fashion for lacquer, porcelain, and decoration incorporating typical Japanese motifs such as masks, dragons, and cranes. Vesta cases such as this one were produced in Japan, and exported; they are characterized by great attention to detail, as seen on the hair and face of this monkey, and a distinctive metalworking technique of combining brass, gold, and copper. Ivory and black enamel inlaid with gold and silver (called zogan) were also favoured materials of Japanese casemakers.

Japanese monkey, 1890s,
£200–300/$320–480

Early vesta cases I

materials: range from the inexpensive, such as tin, brass, and wood, to gold, silver, ivory, hardstones, and tortoiseshell; **small ring:** used to suspend the case from a watch chain, and is common on cases made in England but less so on Continental European and American examples.

▼ Enamelled silver vesta case

As with other types of silver, such as cups and tankards, vesta cases were often specially made as presentation or commemorative gifts, or mementos. This piece, with the front enamelled as a facsimile of a calling card, was given by the Lord Mayor of Leeds to Capt. Alf Cooke J.P., as recorded by an engraved inscription on the back. This piece may not be as valuable as a plain, silver or gold case, as personalized items are less popular with collectors today.

A calling card, H&A of Birmingham, 1897,
£500–600/$800–960

Silver vesta case, by Unger Brothers, late 19thC,
£300–350/$480–560

Gold vesta case, late 19thC,
£400–600/$640–960

Gold vesta case, late 19thC,
£300–400/$480–640

▲ Engraved and gem-set gold vesta case

This American gold vesta case, undoubtedly made for a wealthy customer, as it is set with diamonds and other hardstones, is engraved with a design of, possibly, a Native American woman, and, appropriately, a tobacco plant. Scantily clad women such as this were a favoured design on vesta and cigarette cases in the late 19thC, as the majority of smokers were men. The back of the case has a plain cartouche, which could be engraved with the owner's monogram or initials. Gold and silver cases often had strikers stamped or etched directly into the metal, as on this example.

▲ Silver vesta case

This American vesta case features a finely detailed head of a Native American with headdress; Native Americans were a very popular subject for cases among major silver manufacturers in the United States, such as Unger Brothers, the Gorham Manufacturing Co., and Reed & Barton. On designs in high relief such as this one, check for holes in the metal, as mass-produced designs were often die-stamped from very thin-gauge sheet silver. Unlike British silver vesta cases, which should carry a full set of hallmarks, American silver cases are often just stamped "STERLING" and thus difficult to date accurately.

▲ Diamond-set gold vesta case

Solid gold vesta cases such as this late 19thC American piece are relatively rare today and so can fetch high prices. As with this elegant case studded with diamonds, solid gold items are often simpler in design than cases in other materials; the most common form of decoration is an engraved monogram, and enamelled gold cases are exceptionally rare and valuable. Expensive cases, such as those made of gold, or enamelled, or set with gems, were often made en suite with a cigarette case in the early 20thC. The rounded edges of the case were essential to prevent it from tearing clothing if carried on the person.

Silver vesta case, by Mappin & Webb, 1905, **£150–200/ $240–320**

Silver-plated vesta case, c.1900, **£40–60/$65–95**

Silver vesta case, c.1910, **£650–700/$1,050–1,120**

▲ Silver-plated vesta case

With the advent of commercial advertising in the late 19thC, many manufacturers used vesta cases as vehicles for promoting their products, – as in this case advertising Colman's Mustard. Cases of this type are often plated rather than solid silver, and consequently less expensive. This piece also has a damaged, ill-fitting lid, which would lower its value. A huge range of cases advertising cafés, hotels, food products, and hardware, for example, is available to collectors today. Some boxes have attached glass or plastic "windows" for advertising cards or photographs rather than enamelled decoration.

▲ Enamelled silver vesta case

The popularity of the vesta case in the late 19thC and early 20thC coincided with the advent of new modes of transport such as cars and aeroplanes, which, because of their novelty, were favoured themes of decoration. This case would appeal to the vintage car enthusiast, as well as the specialist vesta case collector. As they were often made of thin metal, and frequently handled, cases such as this one are often dented. Always check for dents in enamelled decoration, as this is extremely difficult to repair.

▲ Silver double-hinged vesta case

This English vesta case has enamelled lids at both ends and two compartments, one for holding vesta matches and the other for fusees. It is essential to check that the hinges on the lids are in good condition, and that lids fit correctly. The ring used to suspend the vesta case from a watch chain is characteristic of cases produced in England, but less common on Continental European pieces.

Lighters pre 1920

Before the late 19thC, numerous implements, such as tinder pistols, and matchlock and flintlock mechanisms, which were developed for 17thC and 18thC weapons, were available for lighting pipes. The most successful method involved striking a flint against steel to produce a spark to light a combustible material that would smoulder gently rather than explode. With the growing fashion for cigar-smoking in the second half of the 19thC, table lighters were much in demand, and were often elaborately decorated, or made in silver or brass novelty designs; portable lighters first appeared in the last decades of the 19thC, when cigarette smoking became popular. The invention in Austria of Auer metal (*see p.60*), in 1903, enabled the development of more efficient lighter mechanisms, leading eventually to the enormous variety of lighters manufactured today.

▶ **Table smokers' compendium**

Ornate novelty shapes for table lighters were especially popular during the late 19thC, and remain so with collectors today. This electroplated example, on a hardstone base, is in the form of a camel carrying a bundle, reflecting the Victorian fashion for detailed naturalism and exotic subject matter. Probably used in a bar or restaurant, it features a central lighter that would be filled with spirit, lit, and left to burn; side lighters with "minaret" covers would be lit from this central flame, and used to light a cigar or pipe.

Table smokers' compendium, c.1870, **£400–450/$640–720**

▼ **Dragon-shaped lighter**

A dragon with one talon raised over a ball was one of the most common Victorian and Edwardian table lighter forms, and was very popular with British Army regiments. This design is made in silver plate and antelope horn. The flame, appropriately, would emerge through the dragon's mouth when the lighter was ignited. The horn handle was sometimes set in a swivelling holder, so that it could be used to pass the lighter around the table.

Dragon-shaped lighter, 1900, **£350–450/$560–720**

Smokers' fashions
The ornate style and large size of many late 19thC table lighters reflected the popularity of smoking among the wealthy; many large country houses had dedicated smoking rooms, where gentlemen would don their velvet jackets and caps while enjoying cigars, or pipes, and conversation.

▼ Shrapnel lighter
During World War I, "trench" lighters were manufactured in large numbers from spent brass shell casings, helmets, coins, and buttons, since brass was in short supply through munitions manufacture. It was often thought that these lighters had been made by soldiers in the trenches; however, they are more likely to have been made by civilians, who gathered the materials from the battlefields, and made the lighters as souvenirs to sell or trade to the soldiers.

Shrapnel lighter, 1914–18, **£15–20/$24–32**

▼ Gondola lighter
This gondola lighter is a particularly unusual design, and so will be valuable if in good condition; many late 19thC and early 20thC table lighters have been subjected to heavy use, and so are frequently damaged. The front part of the gondola holds the spirit oil and wick for lighting cigars or pipes, while the hollow hull could store matches – a match-striker is contained within the deck house. Lighters such as these were often weighted in the bases so that they would return to an upright position if knocked over.

Gondola lighter, 1906, **£2,000–3,000/$3,200–4,800**

▼ Regimental button lighter
The use of buttons and coins was common for small, circular "trench" lighters during World War I. French and American versions often feature patriotic emblems such as, respectively, lions and cockerels and the stars and stripes. Such lighters are much sought after by collectors, but, because of their popularity, are known to have been faked: if a coin is used, always check that the date is no later than 1918.

Regimental button lighter, 1914–18, **£15–20/$24–32**

Cigarette cases pre 1920

Cigarettes developed as an inexpensive alternative to cigars in the mid 19thC; during the Crimean War (1853–6), soldiers from Turkey and Russia introduced them to British and French soldiers, who found it easier and cheaper to roll tobacco in paper tubes than to buy hand-made cigars. Cigarettes were originally sold in thin paper wrappings, so, from the late 19thC, cases were made for carrying them. Cigarette cases are generally square or rectangular; they were produced in gold and silver for the wealthiest smokers, but also in base metal, electroplate, chrome, tortoiseshell, wood, and, in the early 20thC, plastic. They are now usually collected for their decorative appeal, since modern, king-size cigarettes with filters are too large to fit in 19thC and early 20thC cases.

▼ **Russian case**
The most collectable cigarette cases found on the market today are those with fine, enamelled, risqué scenes of nude women; such decoration was a speciality of German and Austrian makers, but this gilt-lined silver case was made in Moscow in 1891. The combination of diamond-set Cyrillic initials – probably those of the owner – and motifs with painted enamels is distinctively Russian. The reverse of the case also has gem-set initials and crowns, indicating that it was probably made for a wealthy aristocrat.

Russian case, 1891,
£600–800/
$960–1,280

▶ **Art Nouveau Continental European silver case**
This silver case was made when the Art Nouveau style reached its height of popularity. The decoration on the lid – a woman's head with flowing hair, set against a background of naturalistic foliage and mistletoe, stylized flowers, and curving, scrolling, gold tendrils – is similar to the famous Art Nouveau theatre posters designed by Alphonse Mucha. The hallmarks indicate that this case was made in Continental Europe, but imported by a retailer for sale in London.

Silver case, 1898,
£300–400/
$480–640

Russian cases: Moscow or St Petersburg?
Moscow: *cloisonné* enamelling, niello, and filigree; characters from Russian folklore, or peasants at work.
St Petersburg: the Neo-classical, characterized by the use of transparent enamels to create textural effects, initials and motifs, and sunray patterns.

Russian case, late 19thC,
£250–300/$400–480

▲ Russian silver-and-niello case

This case has buildings in St Petersburg or Moscow shown on the lid, a style of decoration similar to that of the "castle-top" snuff boxes made in Birmingham, which depicted famous landmarks such as Windsor Castle (see p.16). The images on castle-top boxes are generally cast or die-stamped, but this case uses niello – a decorative technique using a compound of silver, lead, copper, and sulphur applied to designs cut into the metal, and fired to create a lustrous, black surface. This case is oblong rather than square, as Russian cigarettes were longer than European ones.

▼ Russian enamelled silver-gilt case

The enamelled design of a phoenix on the lid of this case represents the resurgence of interest in folk traditions of fantastical warriors and birds in late 19thC Russia. Moscow, where this case was made, was the main centre for the production of silverware in this style, although the scrolling foliage in this design shows the influence of European Art Nouveau. The enamel should be carefully checked for cracks and chips, which will reduce the value.

Russian case, c.1900,
£600–800/$960–1,280

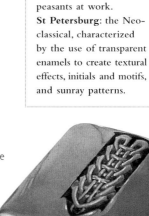

Enamelled silver case, Birmingham, 1903,
£300–400/$480–640

▲ Liberty and Co.

From the 1890s the well-known firm of Liberty and Co., London, sold a wide range of silver items such as cups, bowls, and jewellery with simple, elegant designs influenced by the work of Arts and Crafts designers. The pieces, like this case, are distinguished by the use of interlacing – inspired by Celtic art – and blue-and-green enamelling. With the growing interest in Art Nouveau and Arts and Crafts silver, they have become increasingly collectable.

▼ Fabergé, jewelled, silver-and-gold case

Cigarette cases by Fabergé are among the rarest and most valuable on the market today, and much sought after by collectors. The most luxurious materials are used in this case: gold and silver, with a pushpiece made of a gold-mounted cabochon sapphire, and a diamond-encrusted, gold, double-headed imperial eagle – which may indicate that it was given by or made as a gift for the Tsar and his family. This piece was made by Gabriel Zachariasson Niukkanen, a St Petersburg master goldsmith employed as an outworker by the Fabergé firm, who specialized in gold-and-silver cigarette cases.

Silver and gold case, Fabergé, 1899–1908, £2,000–2,500/ $3,200– 4,000

▼ Austro-Hungarian, gilt-lined, enamelled silver case

The suggestive scene of a partially clad woman is characteristic of the decoration found on cases made in Austria-Hungary during the late 19thC and early 20thC. This image was carefully hidden under a double-hinged lid. The gilt-lined interior visible here would help to protect the silver from corrosion by acid in the tobacco – the cigarettes would have been packed snugly on either side of the case, and held in place by a rubber band, which is now often missing from such cases.

Austro-Hungarian case, c.1910, £700–1,000/$1,120–1,600

▼ English case

The fine, enamelled circus scene on this English case – depicting a blonde girl in a pink tutu, sitting on a white horse which is cantering around the circus ring, while a clown looks on – is quite an unusual subject for a cigarette case, but would be less desirable than one with an enamelled hunting, sporting, or erotic scene. It was made in Birmingham, where vast numbers of small silver items were mass-produced during the 19thC. The circular format of the design is similar to that of some vesta cases – many of these were made to match cigarette cases.

English case, 1896, £200–250/$320–400

Fabergé marks
Fabergé cigarette cases are among the most sought after by collectors. In general all the items made in St Petersburg carry the mark of the firm – Fabergé's name without initials, usually in Cyrillic, or, on small items, the initials "KF" in Cyrillic – combined with the Cyrillic initials of the head of the workshop or the independent craftsman.

▼ **Austro-Hungarian silver case**
The wide variety of cases enamelled with risqué scenes of partially clothed women is a useful indicator of how smoking accessories were intended for men, until smoking became acceptable for women after World War I. This silver case, decorated with an enamelled picture of a girl holding flowers, was made by Georg A. Scheidt; the style of the girl's dress helps to date the piece to the first decade of the 20thC. The rounded corners prevent clothing from being torn while the case is carried in the pocket.

Austro-Hungarian case, Georg A. Scheidt, c.1910, **£400–600/$640–960**

▼ **German silver case**
Many hundreds of cases with enamelled designs were produced in Germany in the late 19thC and early 20thC, as the country experienced a burst of growth in its manufacturing industry after unification in 1871. The fine detailing and rich colours of the enamelled decoration on the lid of this piece, together with its subject, mean that it will fetch a high price.

German case, c.1910, **£800–1,000/$1,280–1,600**

▼ **Fabergé silver case**
The tube shape of this elegant Fabergé case, set with a rose-cut diamond thumbpiece, is more unusual than an oblong or a square shape, making it especially desirable to collectors. The cigarettes inside would have been piled on top of one another. Similar cases use the distinctive technique of *guilloché* enamelling employed by Fabergé – the surface of the metal was mechanically engine-turned in wave-like patterns, and then covered with translucent enamel to create shimmering patterns reminiscent of watered silk.

Silver case, Fabergé, 1915, **£2,000–3,000/$3,200–4,800**

Cigar cases

Cigars were first introduced into Europe from Cuba and North America by the Spanish in the 16thC – a royal cigar-making factory was founded in Spain in 1731. However, cigar-smoking only became popular in the rest of Europe after the Peninsular War in the early 19thC, when British and French soldiers were introduced to the habit while fighting in Spain and Portugal. It soon displaced snuff as the most fashionable way of enjoying tobacco, and cases for carrying cigars were produced by the mid 19thC. These were made in materials similar to snuff boxes, such as wood, horn, and papier mâché, and, for the wealthier, tortoiseshell, silver, ivory, and exotic shagreen, lizard, and crocodile skin, with silver mounts.

Birchwood cigar case, c.1900, **£300–400/ $480–640**

▲ Russian birchwood cigar case
This elegant case, made in richly figured Karelian birchwood, may have been a gift from the Russian imperial family, judging by the jewelled, gold, imperial double-headed eagle in the corner of the lid, and the use of luxurious materials, such as a rose-cut diamond on the thumbpiece. Such cases in fine condition are highly prized by collectors.

▶ English silver "torpedo" cigar case
Most cigar cases were made to hold three or four cigars, but cases for single cigars were also popular during the 19thC, since a cigar was an expensive luxury to be savoured. This example, made in Birmingham, is finely engraved with a pattern of scrolling foliage – similar cases are decorated with embossing, fluting, engine-turning, bright-cutting, or enamelling. It is important to check that the two parts of the case fit snugly together. Single cigar cases such as this sometimes had built-in extinguishers so that smokers did not have to throw away half-smoked cigars.

Silver cigar case, 1902, **£200–300/ $320–480**

Cigar dispensers

These were made in the 19thC and early 20thC, usually of veneered wood, or silver, and designed to stand on a surface. Among the most popular was a drum-shaped container with a central button, which when pressed opened to reveal six cigars.

Leather cigar case, 1876, **£150–170/$240–270**

▲ English leather cigar case with silver mounts

Leather became common in the manufacture of cigar cases, after an inexpensive method of moulding and pressing it was discovered in the 1850s. This severely plain case is typically English, with simple trimming of silver mounts – cases from other parts of Europe are often more lavishly decorated. As the silver is hallmarked it is possible to date this case more accurately than those in other materials, such as wood or papier-mâché. This case is of the "sleeve", rather than the hinged, type, with an inner case to protect the cigars that is inserted at one end.

▼ German wooden cigar case

Wood was the most popular and economical material for cigar cases during the 19thC. Most were decorated with black transfer prints – here, a figure of a pipe smoker. This case is hinged, with a spring catch to keep it firmly closed, to stop the cigars drying out. The corners are rounded to prevent clothing from being torn while the case is carried in the pocket. Unlike cigarette cases – too small for modern cigarettes – cigar cases are still popular with smokers today as they are useful as well as decorative.

Wooden cigar case, c.1850–90, **£225–250/$360–400**

Papier-mâché cigar case, c.1850–90, **£400–440/$640–700**

▲ French cigar case

Decorated cases such as this one, embellished with a finely painted portrait, are more collectable than plain cases. This case is made from two sheets of papier-mâché with curved ends, joined with leather gussets – the cigars were held in a separate case, now often missing from such cases.

Cigarette boxes & tins pre 1914

Before the late 19thC cigarettes were sold loose in paper wrappings – while carrying an essential stock of cigarettes in a small case, the wealthy smoker kept a ready supply at home in a cigarette box. These boxes were generally produced in oblong designs, often in silver with simple, engraved,or engine-turned decoration. Cigarette tins with printed designs advertising the manufacturer or retailer appeared with the introduction of both mass-produced, cheaper cigarettes, and commercially viable lithography, in the 1870s and 1880s. Produced in hundreds of colourful designs – reflecting manufacturers' attempts to create distinctive identities and thus brand loyalty for their cigarettes – these tins are usually the same size as contemporary cigarette cases, but generally much more affordable, as they were made of less expensive materials.

▼ **Russian silver-gilt cigar/cigarette box**
Made by Gustav Klingert, a leading Moscow silversmith, this elegant box is appropriately engraved with designs of tobacco tax bands, imitating the paper labels found on the wooden caddies and crates used for shipping cigars and cigarettes. As in cigarette cases, the interior is gilded, but most cigar and cigarette boxes were lined with cedar to prevent the tobacco drying out.

Malachite cigarette box, 1908–17, **£1,500–2,000/$2,400–3,200**

◀ **Malachite cigarette box**
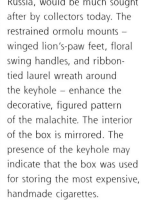
Made from the most luxurious materials, this fine cigarette box, possibly made in Russia, would be much sought after by collectors today. The restrained ormolu mounts – winged lion's-paw feet, floral swing handles, and ribbon-tied laurel wreath around the keyhole – enhance the decorative, figured pattern of the malachite. The interior of the box is mirrored. The presence of the keyhole may indicate that the box was used for storing the most expensive, handmade cigarettes.

Silver-gilt cigar/ cigarette box, Gustav Klingert, Moscow, c.1880, **£1,000–1,500/ $1,600–2,400**

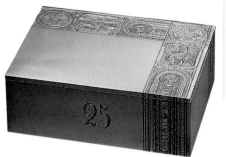

▼ Russian cigarette box

Enamelled designs, although often found on cigarette cases, are relatively rare on cigarette boxes: the lid of this silver-gilt box, with the maker's mark of Samokish, Moscow, features a finely painted enamel plaque of a Russian woman gazing out of a window. Such subjects were favoured by Russian jewellers and silversmiths with the revival of interest in Russian folk art in the late 19thC and early 20thC. Boxes such as this often had movable partitions inside, so that they could accommodate cigars and cigarettes of different sizes.

Russian cigarette box, Samokish, Moscow 1908–17, **£600–800/ $960–1,280**

▼ Cigarette tin

Although most cigarette tins featured advertising for the manufacturer or retailer, some relatively rare tins were produced as souvenirs; this curved one, made for the Yeoward Line shipping company, may have been kept by a traveller as a memento of a long sea voyage. Like cigarette cases, tins were often slim and curved, with rounded corners, to fit easily into a hip pocket, and were sometimes sold with 10 to 20 cigarettes.

Cigarette tin, c.1910, **£120–150/$190–240**

American tobacco packaging

Among the best-known American tobacco brands are R.J. Reynolds's "Camel", launched in 1917, and Lucky Strike, which has a striking, but simple, red "bull's eye" packet, created in 1941, and designed by Richard Loewy (1893–1986).

▼ "Player's Navy Cut" cigarette tin

"Player's Navy Cut", launched by John Player and Sons, became one of the most popular brands of cigarette in the early 20thC, and the style of its packaging exploited the traditional link between sailors and tobacco. The trademark of the sailor's head was introduced in 1883, and the lifebuoy frame dates from 1888. This relatively early design is quite pictorial; later tins of the 1920s and 1930s feature lids in plain colours, with the lifebuoy motif in one corner.

"Player's Navy Cut", c.1910, **£15–20/$24–32**

Cigar piercers, cutters, & holders

From the early 19thC the fashion for cigar-smoking created a demand for a wide range of useful accessories for the smoker. Cigar cutters and piercers appeared in the mid 19thC, with the introduction of larger cigars, and were used to make the cigar draw properly: piercers made a hole, while cutters either snipped off the end of the cigar, or created a V-shaped nick; the purpose was the same, but the method used was dependent upon the individual smoker's taste. Holders for cigars – originally called "cigar tubes" – were also available from this period, and were originally made from clay; late 19thC examples, however, made by pipemakers, were often elaborately carved in meerschaum. Other cigar-related items collected today include cigar moulds, dispensers, and labels or bands.

Cigar piercers, c.1890, **£85–100/ $135–160 each**

 Dutch silver cigar piercers
Like cutters, cigar piercers were often made of steel to prolong their use, but some fine examples were made in gold or silver, and are particularly rare today. Most silver piercers are relatively plain, but these ones have unusual decorative terminals in the shape of an acorn, a ship, and a cow. As they were originally expensive, these piercers would probably have been sold with a leather carrying case.

▼ **Multi-purpose silver cigar cutter**
This item is typical of the late 19thC Victorian fascination with cleverly disguised, ingenious, mechanical devices: made in the form of a chamber candlestick, it has a tube-shaped cutter for removing the end of a cigar, which would drop into the pan. The nozzle holds a candle for lighting the cigar. Devices such as this are more unusual than smaller portable cutters, and so can fetch high prices if in good condition.

Cigar cutter, 1896, **£600–700/ $960–1,120**

Cigar labels

Decorative paper labels or bands for cigars were introduced in the mid 19thC, when Havana cigars began to be exported to Europe on a large scale. Unlike later cigarette cards, they are rarely pictorial, but instead are generally printed, or embossed, in colourful designs, featuring the name of the cigar manufacturer.

Cigar cutter, late 19thC, **£60–80/$95–130**

▲ Brass cigar cutter

Cigar cutters were produced in a huge variety of novelty designs during the late 19thC and early 20thC, especially as miniature figures, animals, heads, and bottles. Like vesta cases, this cutter in the form of a whisky bottle may have been an advertising promotion. Brass examples are more common today than those made in silver or gold. The loop at the top of the cutter would have been used to attach it to a watch chain, but is now useful for hanging the cutter on a keyring.

▼ Cheroot holder

Cheroots were smaller cigars, invented by the Portuguese in India in the late 17thC, and, unlike normal cigars, they are cut flat at both ends. Cheroot and cigar holders were produced in two main forms in the 19thC: a straight tube shape, like this holder, or an elaborate, S-shaped, curved style. This holder typically features an amber mouthpiece, and decorative gold bands, with gold wire decoration around the carved meerschaum tube. The original case for the holder will add value. Similar, tube-shaped, high-quality holders were made from porcelain, lacquered wood, and carved ivory.

Cheroot holder, made in Budapest, 1840, **£220–250/$350–400**

Cigar holder, probably Austrian, c.1895, **£70–80/ $110–130**

▲ Cigar holder

Elaborately carved meerschaum cigar holders were a speciality of Austrian (particularly Viennese), French, and German pipe makers during the late 19thC, and so generally follow the style of contemporary meerschaum pipes. However, they can be distinguished from pipes by the small, detachable bowl for holding the cigar at the end. Like most high-quality meerschaum holders, this has an amber mouthpiece, but some rare mouthpieces are made of tortoiseshell.

Pipes

Most familiar to collectors today is the clay pipe, first produced in The Netherlands and England in the early 17thC – demand for these eventually became so high that during the 18thC and 19thC millions were produced every year. The price of clay pipes was very low, so everyone could afford them. In the 19thC, many high-quality pipes in unusual and elaborate designs were created by pipe manufacturers, to compete with the widespread new fashion for cigars and, later, cigarettes. These included finely carved meerschaum and wooden pipes – a speciality of central European pipemakers – and figural clay pipes from France. Such items are especially collectable today, and there is also much interest among collectors in ethnographic pipes from Africa, Japan, and China.

▼ **Native American micmac pipe and tobacco pouch**

Most Native American pipes are tube-like, rather than with the curved stem familiar in European pipes. This type of pipe, with a vase-shaped bowl, and keel-like base, developed among the Plains Ojibwa, Cree, Blackfoot, and Micmac peoples. The stem was made separately of soft wood, and decorated with beadwork in a striped pattern; other examples are adorned with fur or horsehair.

Micmac pipe and tobacco pouch, c.1800, **£220–250/ $350–400**

▼ **English glass pipe**

Glass pipes were made as decorative pieces, and never intended for smoking. Such pipes were produced by glassworkers, along with bells, walking sticks, flasks, rolling pins, and other small items, from the molten glass left at the end of the day. Popular from the 1850s, these pipes are associated with the Nailsea Glasshouse, but were also made at other glassworks in and around Bristol in England. The looped pattern is characteristic, as are the bulbous stem and tulip-shaped bowl.

English glass pipe, c.1900, **£160–180/ $250–290**

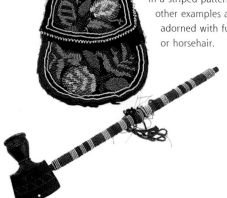

▼ German wooded pipe

This exquisitely carved wooden pipe – a speciality of German makers – was formerly in the collection of William Bragge (1823–84), a wealthy Sheffield steel manufacturer, who in the mid 19thC assembled a famous collection of over 7,000 pipes, and other wares, relating to tobacco- and opium-smoking. His collection was auctioned in 1882, and dispersed around the world. The tiny, carved pinnacles and crockets on the stem represent the influence of the revival of the Gothic architectural style in the 1840s. The silver bands and bowl lid will be hallmarked, and this will help to date the pipe.

German wooden pipe, c.1846, **£550–600/ $880–960**

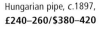
Hungarian pipe, c.1897, **£240–260/$380–420**

▲ Hungarian pipe

The extremely long and narrow, cylindrical pipe bowl is characteristic of pipes made in central Europe, and particularly in Hungary, Bulgaria, and Romania. The bowl is ceramic, while the stem is wooden. Such pipes are often decorated with finely incised, geometric patterns, and have very short, sloping ends on the bowls, with collars for securing the stems.

Briar pipes

Briar is the wood of the heath tree growing on the Mediterranean coast. It was allegedly discovered by a pipemaker visiting Corsica, who broke his meerschaum pipe and had a replacement made from briar; he took back samples to establish the briar-pipemaking industry in the Jura region of France. It is only pipes in fine condition or by a well-known maker that will be valuable.

FACT FILE

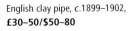
English clay pipe, c.1899–1902, **£30–50/$50–80**

▲ English clay pipe

During the 19thC, pipe bowls decorated with, or formed as, portraits of famous contemporary figures were popular in France, and later England. This clay pipe, made during the Boer War, features a likeness of General Baden-Powell on one side of the bowl, and of General Sir George White on the other. The mark of Charles Cropp & Sons of London, one of the leading 19thC British pipemakers, is stamped along the stem. The small "spur" under the bowl was introduced in the 18thC.

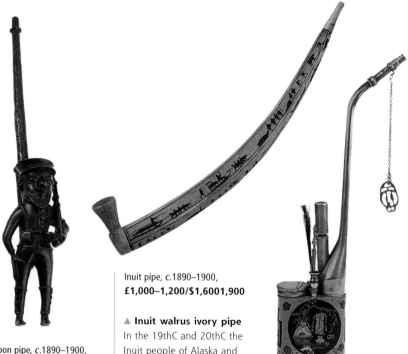

Cameroon pipe, c.1890–1900,
£750–850/$1,200–1,350

Inuit pipe, c.1890–1900,
£1,000–1,200/$1,6001,900

Chinese pipe, 19thC,
£80–100/$130–160

▲ **West African brass pipe**
Tobacco was introduced into
West Africa by European traders
and settlers in the 17thC.
Pipes were smoked by both
men and women of various
peoples, particularly in the
Cameroon highlands, and the
size, material, and decoration
of a pipe indicated the owner's
wealth and status. While
many pipes in clay, terracotta,
wood, ivory, and metal
were fashioned as fantastic
animals or masks – reflecting
indigenous artistic traditions –
some were inspired by
colonial life. The bowl of this
Cameroon brass pipe depicts a
European soldier with his rifle.

▲ **Inuit walrus ivory pipe**
In the 19thC and 20thC the
Inuit people of Alaska and
northern Canada carved
decorated pipes from walrus
ivory for commercial sale –
before European contact,
pipes were generally plain
and functional. This typical
example features miniature
scenes of the Inuit hunting
whales, walrus, and caribou,
and has a curved stem. The
tiny bowl of the pipe is similar
to that on Asian pipes.

▲ **Chinese water pipe**
Popular throughout Asia,
the Middle East, and Africa,
the water pipe consists of a
container of water to which
the mouthpiece and a dish or
bowl containing the burning
tobacco is attached. The
tobacco smoke passes through
the water into the mouth-
piece, cooling it, and filtering
impurities such as dust.
The Chinese invented a small
portable version, which was
generally decorated with fine
cloisonné enamel. The top of
this pipe also carries a small
brush for removing ash.

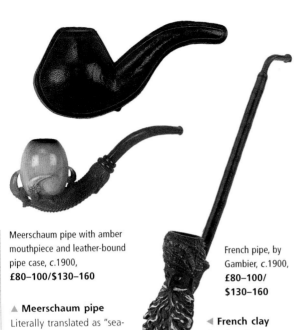

Porcelain pipes

Pipes were manufactured by major European porcelain factories, such as Meissen and Nymphenburg, from the early 18thC. Porcelain pipes were made in three parts: a long mouthpiece, a slender, upright bowl, and a Y-shaped reservoir, in which tobacco juices collected, since glazed porcelain was non-absorbent.

Meerschaum pipe with amber mouthpiece and leather-bound pipe case, c.1900,
£80–100/$130–160

French pipe, by Gambier, c.1900,
£80–100/ $130–160

Dutch pipe, by Goedwaagen of Gouda, c.1940,
£50–60/ $80–95

▲ Meerschaum pipe

Literally translated as "sea-foam", meerschaum is a silicate of magnesia that was first discovered on the shores of the Black Sea, and was indeed originally believed to be petrified sea-foam. From the mid 18thC it became a popular medium for pipe bowls, since it could be carved easily, and turned an attractive, deep yellow-amber in colour when tobacco was smoked through it. Most meerschaum pipes were made in Germany and Austria, particularly Vienna: the eagle's talon motif on this bowl represented part of the Austrian imperial emblem. Such designs are more affordable than the elaborately carved human and animal heads and figures also made in the 19thC.

◀ French clay pipe bowl

The firm of Gambier of Givet and Paris was one of three major French pipe manufacturers in the second half of the 19thC; the others were Dumeril and Fiolet. All three produced thousands of different, figural clay pipe bowls, representing famous politicians, actors, and writers; mythological characters; animals; and copies of ancient sculpture. This "Jacob" pipe – typically with traces of enamel painting – was made by Gambier in up to 14 sizes. The popularity of such pipe bowls meant that they were widely copied by Dutch, German, and Belgian makers in the late 19thC and early 20thC.

▲ Dutch red clay pipe

This amusing modern pipe features miniature figures of a family and its dog along the stem, and is inscribed "The Whole Dam Family". From the 17thC Gouda has been the leading pipemaking centre in The Netherlands, and pipes made there are generally easier to identify, as makers were required to register a mark (stamped on the heel of the pipe) – initials, a personal emblem, or, from the 18thC, a number surmounted by a crown – with the city's pipemakers' guild.

Pipe cases, tobacco tampers, & pouches

Clay and meerschaum pipes are particularly fragile, and, from the beginning of pipe-smoking in 16thC Europe, cases were made to protect them. In the 19thC and early 20thC, elaborately carved meerschaum and other pipes had pine-wood cases, covered with leather (*see p.43*), and lined with velvet. The pipe smoker also needed to carry a sufficient supply of tobacco, usually in a box, but sometimes in a pouch. Stoppers, or tampers, were needed to press down the burning tobacco in the pipe bowl. These were carved from bone, wood, ivory, and horn, although some rare examples in pottery, porcelain, glass, and mother of pearl have also been found.

◄ Tortoiseshell pipe case
Most pipe cases are easily identified, as they are generally shaped as pipes; the size of the part containing the bowl can help in dating, since early pipes had small bowls. This rare and valuable case would have been made for a wealthy smoker, as tortoiseshell was a highly prized, and expensive, material. It is particularly collectable, as it contains an early clay pipe.

Tortoiseshell pipe case,
£1,800–2,000/$2,900–3,200

▼ Dutch carved wooden pipe case
The fashion for smoking clay pipes in The Netherlands is evident in the many 17thC and 18thC Dutch paintings of domestic life, and some of the most elaborate pipe cases are Dutch. The bowl part of this case is richly carved in the form of a lion's head; some cases depict human heads. English cases are generally much simpler, and plainer in style.

Wooden pipe case, 1739,
£2,000–2,500/$3,200–4,000

Pipe holders

When not in use, pipes were often stored at home in pipe racks. The simplest type, attached horizontally to the wall and intended for fragile clay pipes, consisted of a wooden board, pierced with holes, on which the bowls sat. Some desk holders combine a pipe rack with a candlestick and/or ashtray.

▼ Japanese pipes (*kiseru*) and cases

Tobacco was brought to Japan by Europeans in the 17thC; the Japanese developed a taste for very fine, heavy tobacco, smoked in very small amounts, as shown by the tiny metal bowls of their pipes. However, the finely carved pipe cases, made of expensive materials such as ivory and staghorn, are now much more collectable than the pipes. The designs were probably created by professional carvers, who would also have carved *netsuke* (see p.61).

19thC; pipes **£35–45/$55–70 each**, staghorn case (right) & ivory case (left) **£700–800/$1,120–1,280 each**

Native American pouch, **£300–500/ $480–800**

Tampers, late 19thC, **£50–60/$80–95 each**

▲ Tobacco tampers: ivory boot, brass bust, and wooden shoe

Used from the early 17thC, pipe tampers were decorative as well as useful; most were shaped like arms or legs, although heads of famous figures, such as Nelson and Napoleon, were also produced. The diameter of the base of a tamper is a useful guide to dating: the smaller the size, the earlier the date, since tampers were designed to fit into the narrow bowls of early pipes. Many fine ones of wood, ivory, or bone are capped at the bottom with silver or pewter to prevent charring. Some hollow tampers contain a small steel pin, or pricker, for removing ash from the bowl.

▲ Native American pouch

Tobacco pouches have been produced in an variety of shapes and styles for smokers throughout the world. Most surviving European examples are made of leather or silk, the latter sometimes richly embroidered by women as a gift to a male smoker. This Native American Blackfoot buckskin pouch is decorated around the rim, and down one side, with a band of sky blue, navy, red, and yellow beads, and with beadwork panels of chevrons on each side.

Art Deco

The Art Deco style of the 1920s and 1930s was the first distinctively modern style of the 20thC, and was characterized by bold colours, stylized figure and animal motifs, and geometric patterns. Glamorized by Hollywood film stars, smoking reached its height of popularity in this era, and, with increased liberation for women after World War I, it became acceptable for women to smoke in public. The rise of advertising and product branding led to increased competition between cigarette manufacturers, while a number of firms expanded into the production or retailing of luxury smoking accessories, particularly cigarette cases, boxes, and lighters, to meet ever-growing demand. For the less wealthy smoker, accessories were available in a wide range of new materials, such as Bakelite. All Art Deco items are very collectable today.

▼ **English enamelled silver cigarette case**
During the 1920s the most progressive Art Deco designs were produced in France, and in England most smoking accessories were made in styles popular at the turn of the century. The *guilloché* enamelling on the lid of this case, for example, was a type of decoration used earlier by Fabergé. It is overpainted, in enamel, with naturalistic flowers and leaves in muted colours; such items are more affordable today than cases with typically Art Deco geometric patterns.

Enamelled silver cigarette case, 1920s, **£100–150/$160–240**

Silver-gilt cigarette case, 1920s–1930s, **£250–300/$400–480**

◄ **Silver-gilt cigarette case**
The zigzag on this case is among the most distinctive of Art Deco patterns – other typical motifs include chevrons, arrows, and sunbursts. This pattern is enamelled, but examples with similar patterns are often engine-turned, embossed, or engraved, and sometimes feature a shield, or panel, for an engraved monogram. The use of high-quality decorative techniques, such as gilding and enamelling, indicates that this item would originally have been fairly expensive, and will retain its value today.

▼ Cigarette case

With its motif of an aeroplane flying over mountains, the decoration on this case reflects the 1930s preoccupation with speed, travel, and leisure, and fascination with new forms of transport. The bold colours characteristic of Art Deco were influenced by the bright hues of contemporary Fauvist paintings, while abstract Futurist and Cubist paintings inspired the use of angular, stylized forms. Cigarette cases with striking, black-and-white enamel designs are also common today, but less popular with collectors than those with coloured enamel decoration.

Cigarette case, 1920s–1930s,
£300–400/$480–640

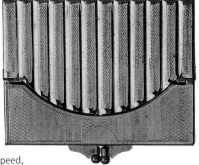

Gold-plated cigarette case,
1920s, **£60–80/$95–130**

▲ Gold-plated cigarette case

During the early 20thC, when smoking became acceptable for women, manufacturers of smoking accessories started to produce items intended specifically for the female smoker: this gold-plated case, with a clip opening and ridges for holding the cigarettes in place, is made in the style of a purse or an evening bag. Such cases were sometimes supplied with elegant silk, or beaded, carrying cases. Women's cigarette cases were frequently smaller than men's.

Some famous makers & brands

FACT FILE

Colibri: lighters with distinctive outside levers; when one is pushed down it opens the top of the lighter, when released it creates the spark; **Thorens:** high-quality lighters with precision mechanisms; **Evans Case Company & the Elgin Manufacturing Company:** Art Deco lighters and cigarette cases.

▼ Cigarette case

Makers of Art Deco cases often used exotic materials, such as ivory, shagreen, lacquer, gold and silver leaf and inlay, and ostrich or alligator skin to create a luxurious but understated effect: this elegant case is inlaid with a simple, "webbed" design in silver. Such cases were often made and sold with a matching lighter (sometimes in a presentation case).

Silver cigarette case, 1920s,
£85–90/$135–145

▼ English silver cigarette box

Boxes for storing a supply of cigarettes on a desk or table at home were especially popular with the unprecedented spread of cigarette-smoking in the 1920s and 1930s. Most are rectangular and fairly plain, but this unusual example has a sprung handle, and two compartments. The hinges of the compartments should always be in premium condition. Such items are sometimes sold today as jewellery boxes, and lined with velvet rather than the original cedarwood, which kept the contents fresh.

Silver cigarette box, made in London, 1928, **£900–1,000/$1,440–1,600**

▼ Silver cigarette box

The "stepped" form of this rectangular cigarette box was a favourite design of Art Deco silversmiths, perhaps inspired by the shape of new American skyscrapers built at this time. The simple, engine-turned border, and the panel on the lid for the monogram of the owner, are particularly common on Art Deco silver boxes. Simple boxes of this type are less popular with collectors today than those with enamelled geometric patterns, and can be quite affordable in good condition.

Silver cigarette box, 1920s–1930s, **£150–200/$240–320**

▼ Alfred Dunhill lighter compact

In the 1920s, the firm of Alfred Dunhill was the leading English retailer of luxury smoking accessories, made in gold, silver, and enamel. Their fine craftsmanship, and typically Art Deco designs, mean that all Alfred Dunhill products are much sought after today. This lighter compact, made for the fashionable female smoker, combines a cigarette lighter, powder compact, and lipstick holder.

Alfred Dunhill lighter compact, c.1927, **£600–800/$960–1,280**

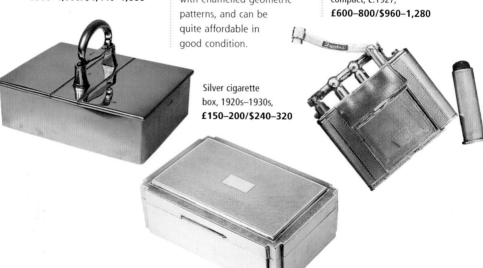

Minaudières
In the 1920s and 1930s, the minaudière, or carryall, was one of the most stylish accessories for the female smoker. It was a large, rectangular or square case, fitted with compartments for face powder, rouge, lipstick, cigarettes, mirror, and a lighter. The most expensive versions were made by the leading jewellers, Cartier, Tiffany, Fouquet, Templier, and Van Cleef & Arpels.

▼ Alfred Dunhill "Unique" watch lighter
The "Unique" watch lighter was introduced in 1926 as a result of a specific request from a South American client, who wanted to combine a timepiece with his Alfred Dunhill "Unique" lighter. The finished article was so appealing that it was put into production, and subsequently became one of the firm's most popular items during the late 1920s and the 1930s. It has since become highly collectable, and many turn up at auctions, fairs, etc. They were made in gold, silver, and silver with enamel, and, in addition, there is the sports version, which has the windshield (see p.50) around the wick.

Alfred Dunhill "Unique" watch lighter, from late 1920s to 1930s, **£800–1,200/$1,280–1,900**

▼ Ronson table lighter
The Ronson firm, of Newark, New Jersey, was the first to introduce a fully automatic pocket cigarette lighter – the "Banjo" – in 1926-7, and later became well known for its series of Art Deco novelty, or figurative, table lighters, in black enamel and chrome. This design, known as the "Pudding Bearer", or "Ballerina", features a typically dynamic Art Deco female dancer holding a "Rondelight Baby" petrol and flint lighter. This design has been manufactured in the USA since 1935.

"Pudding Bearer" or "Ballerina", 1930s design, **£400–600/$640–960**

▼ Ronson table lighter
During the Art Deco period, cigarette boxes and lighters were often combined to make stylish, yet functional, table or desk accessories, such as this novelty penguin "Pic-a-Cig" lighter made in chrome-plated and enamelled brass and spelter. When two buttons on the box are pressed, a cigarette is dispensed and lifted by the beak of the penguin.

"Pic-a-Cig", 1930s design, **£500–600/$800–960**

Alfred Dunhill Ltd

World famous for its high-quality luxury goods and smoking accessories, Alfred Dunhill Ltd was founded in London in 1893 by Alfred Dunhill (1872–1959), originally as a motoring accessories business. In the first decade of the 20thC, it expanded into the manufacture and retail of luxury smoker's accessories. In an era when smoking was the height of fashion, the firm met with great success, and opened new shops in Paris, New York, and Toronto in the 1920s. From the 1930s onwards, it expanded into writing instruments and stationery, toiletries, and menswear, but among collectors of smoking accessories Alfred Dunhill is synonymous with finely crafted lighters in the Art Deco style, especially the "Unique", and watch lighters made with solid or plated silver or gold cases.

◀ **Windshield pipe**
Pipes were among the first Alfred Dunhill products; the patent for the windshield pipe was submitted in 1904, and the first "Alfred Dunhill's Patent Shield Pipe" was sold in 1906. This type of briar pipe (see p.41) features a bowl whose end is raised, to make lighting the pipe easier out of doors. Like other early Alfred Dunhill products, such as "face shields", gauntlets, petrol cans, and shower-proof jackets, such pipes were designed specifically to appeal to motorists.

Windshield pipe, c.1913,
£500–600/
$800–960

▼ **Ladies' pipe collection**
Alfred Dunhill was one of the first British firms to offer accessories aimed at the female smoker, including, in its 1920 catalogue, ladies' pipes. Items such as this pipe, with interchangeable long and short mouthpieces and bowls, in its original case, were sold alongside other luxury items such as vanity cases.

Ladies' pipe collection, c.1927,
£1,800–2,000/
$2,900–3,200

Golf ball lighter, 1927,
£800–1,000/$1,280–1,600

▲ **Golf ball lighter**
As well as its renowned
"Unique" lighter (*see above
right*) in stylish, Art Deco
geometric designs, Alfred
Dunhill produced a wide
range of lighters in novelty
forms. This large lighter in
the form of a golf ball was
designed for table rather than
pocket use, and was weighted
in the bottom, so that it
always returned to an upright
position if knocked over.
Golf ball lighters can be more
expensive than other Alfred
Dunhill novelty lighters, as
they will appeal to specialist
collectors of golf-related items.

▼ **Hunting-horn lighter**
The novelty hunting-horn
lighter was introduced in
1932, and the Alfred Dunhill
catalogue of that year
described it as: "An exact
replica of the real thing.
Inverted in the hand it
automatically presents a
light; and replaced on the
table it is once again a
hunting horn."; when the
lighter was turned upside-
down, a weight inside
dropped, activating the
striking mechanism. Unlike
the most expensive Alfred
Dunhill lighters, produced
in silver, gold, enamel, and
lacquer, this type of lighter
is made of brass.

Hunting-horn lighter,
1934, £200–250/$320–400

"Unique" lighter
The "Unique" was
developed by Alfred
Dunhill in conjunction
with F. Wise and W.
Greenwood, and could
be lit easily, one hand
being used to flick a
single wheel. It was first
sold as the "Every-Time" in
1923, and was relaunched
as the "Unique" in 1924.
In 1931 a double-wheel
mechanism was introduced
– the single-wheel
version is now rarer.

Tinder pistol lighter, 1938,
£80–100/$130–160

▲ **Tinder pistol lighter**
The Alfred Dunhill tinder
pistol novelty lighter is based
on the shape of 17thC and
18thC tinder pistol lighters. In
this version when the trigger
is pulled, the top of the
lighter opens, and the wick is
lit by the striking mechanism.
This 1930s model is a petrol-
and-flint lighter, but a gas
version – much rarer today –
was produced in the 1960s.

A l f r e d   D u n h i l l   L t d ~ 51

Zippo

One of the world's best-selling lighters, the Zippo is instantly recognizable by its simple, rectangular, chrome-plated casing, large serrated wheel, and the distinctive "clip" of its hinged lid. The Zippo Manufacturing Company was founded in 1933, and produced a reliable, easy to use, and relatively inexpensive lighter. The Zippo attracts specialist collectors owing to its enormous variety of decoration: from company logos, military and fraternal insignia, and designs commemorating such events as battles and space flights, to scenes of birds, animals, and plants. Among lighters the Zippo is unique in having featured, since 1957, a coding system of dots and slashes on the bottom, indicating the year of manufacture – an invaluable dating tool for collectors.

Reveler lighter, 1930s,
£1,700–2,200/
$2,800–3,500

▶ **Reveler lighter**
Zippo lighters with applied designs, known as "metalliques", were produced from 1935 to 1940, and are much sought after by collectors today. The term "metallique" refers to a very thin sheet of chrome-plated brass, cut into a specified design, and attached to the lighter case. This design is known as the "Reveler"; other well-known metallique patterns included a commemorative image of the 1939 New York World's Fair. The sharp, square corners are typical of a Zippo made in the mid 1930s; later cases have rounded corners.

▼ **Town & Country pocket lighter**
Produced in the 1950s, the Town & Country lighters are among the most sought after Zippo. Town & Country refers to an elaborate method of enamel decoration, in which the basic design is engraved on the case, and the colours then airbrushed onto the lighter one at a time, and fired to build up the design. The value generally depends on the number of colours used. Early Town & Country models tended to feature designs inspired by nature, such as ducks, trout, lily ponds, horses, and Irish setters.

Town & Country, 1950s,
£190–450/$300–720

▼ Moon Landing pocket lighter

Designs on Zippo lighters have often commemorated important US and world events. This lighter, celebrating the Apollo 11 moon landing in 1969, was the last to be produced using the "Town & Country" method of enamel decoration, and is particularly prized by Zippo collectors. Most 1960s Town & Country lighters have fewer colours than in the 1950s versions, and, like the earlier versions, are rarely found in good condition.

Moon Landing, 1969,
£130–160/$200–250

"Elvis", 1987, **£65–95/$105–150**

▲ Elvis lighter

In the 1970s, 1980s, and 1990s, Zippo introduced a new series of designs, commemorating such events as the American Bicentennial of 1976, and the 50th anniversary of the company (1982), as well as honouring famous personalities. This lighter, with a portrait and facsimile signature of Elvis Presley, first appeared in the year of the 10th anniversary of his death. While lighters that were put into production, such as this one, are highly collectable, those with prototype designs, created by the company's art and design department, are extremely rare and valuable.

▼ Varga Girl lighter

From 1992 Zippo introduced a special series of "Collectables of the Year": limited editions of specific designs, intended to appeal particularly to lighter collectors. This design of 1993 features the "Varga Girl" – an Art Deco-style image of a windswept girl lighting her cigarette with a Zippo – who was used in the company's earliest advertising, in the 1930s. This piece should not be confused with a highly valuable, original Zippo of the 1930s, as this design was never used on its earliest lighters.

Varga girl lighter, 1993,
£55–65/ $90–105

Ashtrays & cigar bowls

Now everyday domestic items, dishes or bowls for collecting ash from cigars or cigarettes only appeared after the expansion of the tobacco industry in the mid 19thC. In the 18thC, pipe smokers used an ashes pan – a copper bowl, with three or four legs, and a wooden handle, so that it could be passed around the table. Early ashtrays made specifically for the purpose were often plain and functional, and made from earthenware, electroplated nickel silver, or die-stamped sheet silver, in the prevailing styles of the day, but, from the 1880s, inexpensive glass or metal versions were often used as a medium for advertising. Of most interest to collectors today are those by famous craftsmen or designers.

▼ **French *pâte-de-cristal* glass ashtray**

Gabriel Argy-Rousseau (1885–1953) was one of the principal exponents of the ancient *pâte-de-verre* and *pâte-de-cristal* glassmaking techniques, which were revived in early 20thC France by independent glassmakers, working in the Art Nouveau and Art Deco styles. This green and blue ashtray, in the form of a flowerhead with curling leaves, is typical of his early, Art Nouveau naturalistic style – his later, Art Deco pieces feature stylized figures, geometric patterns, and Egyptian motifs.

Argy-Rousseau glass ashtray, early 20thC, **£700–900/ $1,120–1,440**

Alfred Dunhill ashtray, 1930s, **£50–70/$80–110**

◀ **Alfred Dunhill ashtray**

Designs from the 1930s are much in demand with collectors today, with the resurgence of interest in the Art Deco style. This piece, retailed by Alfred Dunhill, was probably mass-produced, and bought in large quantities by corporate institutions, such as banks, for use in their offices; like modern ashtrays, it features "V"-shaped grooves for propping up the cigarette. Such pieces are less expensive, and easier to obtain, than hand-crafted items, or those by famous designers.

Modern ashtrays
There is increasing interest among collectors in fine-quality, heavy, press-moulded, coloured glass ashtrays from the former Czechoslovakia. Briar ashtrays were also made in limited numbers in Saint Claude, France, before World War II; intended to complement briar pipes, these were made from sliced briar root, and had baize bases.

Silver-and-enamel ashtray, 1943,
£300–400/$480–640

▲ **English silver-and-enamel ashtray**
This square ashtray, with London hallmarks for 1943, is probably quite rare, given the restrictions on the manufacture of silverware and other luxury items during World War II. As with vesta and cigarette cases, its enamelled decoration (in blue, turquoise, and yellow) would make it more appealing to collectors than a plain or engraved piece. It is decorated with floral motifs, and so may have been made for a female smoker.

▼ **Marianne Brandt ashtrays**
Brandt (1893–1983) was one of the best-known metalworkers associated with the Bauhaus school of design. Many Bauhaus designs have now been licensed to modern manufacturers; these repros are made of stainless steel and/or polished brass, but an original piece would have been made of brass or nickel-silver.

Two-piece ashtrays, 1990s repros by Alessi. Below: designed 1926, **£55–60/$90–95**; below left: designed 1924, **£35–40/$55–65**

▼ **Silver cigar bowl**
The curving form, angular supports, and naturalistic cigar rests, in the form of cicadas with outstretched wings, on this cigar bowl are typical of the distinctive style of the Italian Art Nouveau designer Carlo Bugatti. He is generally associated with furniture design, but became interested in silver after moving from Milan to Paris in 1904; like this piece, his metalwork designs were manufactured by the Parisian firm of A.A. Hébrard.

Carlo Bugatti cigar bowl, c.1900, **£600–800/$960–1,280**

Lighters post 1940

Demand for an inexpensive and reliable lighter after World War II gave rise to two inventions: the butane gas lighter, and the disposable lighter. The gas one, launched in 1947, was based on the premise that butane gas is liquid under pressure, and can be kept in a lighter storage tank; the pressure is controlled by a valve in the lighter mechanism, which makes the fuel tank independent of the lighter mechanism. The separate, refillable fuel tank/case inspired the development (for petrol as well as gas lighters) of the disposable model. Despite these developments in gas lighters, petrol ones remained dominant in the postwar market, and a huge range of novelty designs, especially those made in Japan, is collected today.

Alfred Dunhill Roman lamp lighter, c.1952, **£50–80/ $80–130**

▲ **Roman lamp' lighter by Alfred Dunhill**
The design of this Roman lamp table lighter with a serpent handle, harks back to lighters of similar shapes made in the Victorian and Edwardian eras. Alfred Dunhill first introduced this novelty design in 1937, but a modified version was launched in 1952. The lighter was produced in various materials, such as chromium, to suit different tastes and pockets. Like all the Alfred Dunhill lighters shown here, this is a petrol lighter.

▼ **Aquarium lighter by Alfred Dunhill**
From the 1950s, new plastics and colourful motifs were introduced in lighter designs, reflecting the new optimism after wartime destruction. First made in 1950, the "Aquarium" has a perspex case and silver-plated brass mechanism. The three-dimensional effect was created by carving and painting the reverse of the plastic; early cases are said to have been made from the perspex windows of decommis-sioned De Havilland aircraft. Sir Winston Churchill had one of these lighters on his desk while writing his memoirs.

Alfred Dunhill Aquarium lighter, early 1950s, **£600–800/ $960–1,280**

Pipe lighters

Pipe-smoking enjoyed a revival from the mid-20thC. Among the most successful, and now collectable, pipe lighter was the "jet stream" lighter sold by Beattie Jet Products, Inc., of New York from 1945 to the 1960s.

Japanese aeroplane, 1940s, **£170–190/$270–300**

▲ Japanese aeroplane lighter

Although lighters had been produced in Japan since the 1920s, the Japanese lighter industry expanded rapidly during the occupation of Japan by US troops from 1945 to 1952. Thousands of novelty lighters, disguised as miniature consumer goods, such as radios, aeroplanes, typewriters, cameras, and soda bottles – perhaps inspired by the various items imported from home for the soldiers – were produced. These became so popular that major European manufacturers made similar designs – an aeroplane lighter, known as the "Jet Plane lighter", was introduced by Alfred Dunhill c.1952.

▼ "Baby Sylph" lighter by Alfred Dunhill

The elegant "Sylph" was a tall and slim lighter, fitted with the "Unique" mechanism (see p.51), introduced in 1953, and intended particularly to appeal to the female smoker; this miniature version, about 2.5cm/1in high, launched at the same time, could fit conveniently in the smallest evening bag. Most of these lighters were made with gold- or silver-plated cases, but some very expensive, and rare, versions were produced in solid gold or silver.

Alfred Dunhill "Baby Sylph" lighter, 1953,
£400–500/$640–800

Japanese microphone lighter c.1945, **£220–250/$350–400**

▲ Microphone lighter

Even though the US occupation of Japan had ended in 1952, novelty lighters were made in their thousands in the 1960s. Although originally inexpensive, Japanese models were renowned for their fine craftsmanship, and are becoming increasingly collectable today. Examples from 1945 to 1952 are usually stamped "Made in Occupied Japan", though many were assembled and sold in the USA.

Where to see

MAJOR MUSEUMS
Alfred Dunhill Museum
48 Jermyn Street
St James's, London
SW1Y 6LX, England
tel: 0207 290 8600

Ceramic Museum
29 rue Charles-Lapierre
Ardenne, Belgium

Imperial War Museum
Lambeth Road
London SE1 6HZ, England
tel: 0207 416 5000
(especially World War I lighters,
World War II cigarette packets)

Lighter Museum of Holland
Postbus 5670 AA Nuenen
The Netherlands

Musee SEITA
12 Rue Surcrouf
Paris 75007, France
tel: 1 4556 6017
(official French museum
of tobacco)

National Lighter Museum
107 South 2nd St
Guthrie
OK 73044, USA
tel: 405 282 3025

**Pijpenkabinet, Galerie
and Musee**
Prinsengracht 488
1017 KH Amsterdam
The Netherlands
tel: 20 421 1779

Pipe Museum
1 bis rue Cambetta
Saint-Claude, France
tel: 3 8445 1700

Pipe Museum
Via de Chiostro 1/3
Gavirate, Italy

Niemeyer Museum
Brugstraat 24
Groningen, Holland

Tobacco Museum
Maison Peyrarède
Place de Feu
Bergerac, France

Victoria and Albert Museum
Cromwell Road
London SW7 2RL,
England
tel: 0207 942 2000
(especially snuff boxes,
tobacco boxes)

Wervik – Taback Museum
63 Koestraat
Brikkenmolen, Belgium

W.Ø. Larsen (pipe museum)
9 Amagertorv
Copenhagen, Denmark

SPECIALIST CLUBS
AND SOCIETIES
Alliance of Pipe Clubs
c/o McGahey, (for tobacconist)
245 High Street
Exeter, Devon EX4 3NZ
England

**Confrérie of Master
Pipemakers**
42 rue de Pré
39299 Saint-Claude, France

International Pipe Academy
1, Avenue Rober Schuman
75347 Paris, France

Lighter Club of Great Britain
351A Whitehorse Road
Croydon, Surrey CR0 2HS,
England

On the Lighter Side
International Lighters
Collectors
136 Circle Drive
Quitman
TX 75783-0536, USA

Pipe Club of France
c/o 9, rue Saint-Fiacre
75002 Paris, France

**Pocket Lighter Preservation
Guild**
11220 W. Florissant
#400, Florissant
MO 63033, USA

What to read

Bace, Jill *Collecting Silver: The Facts at Your Fingertips,* Miller's, London, 1999

Beaver, Patrick *The Match Makers,* Henry Melland, London, 1985

Bisconcini, Stefano *Lighters,* translated by Mimmio Mancio, Edizioni San Gottardo, Milan, (n.d.)

Brener, Carol & Brener, Stephen W. *Matchsafes in the Collection of the Cooper-Hewitt Museum,* Cooper-Hewitt Museum, New York, 1981

Cage, Deborah & Marsh, Madeleine *Tobacco Containers and Accessories: Their Place in Eighteenth Century European Social History,* Gage, Bluett and Company, London, 1988

Congdon-Martin, Douglas *Tobacco Tins: A Collector's Guide,* Schiffer Publishing Ltd, Atglen, PA, 1992

Urban K. Cummings/ Ronson Corporation *Ronson: The World's Greatest Lighter,* Bird Dog Books, Palo Alto, California, 1992

Delieb, Eric *Investing in Silver,* Barrie & Rockliff, London, 1967

Ettinger, Roseann *Compacts and Smoking Accessories,* Schiffer Publishing, West Chester, PA, 1991

Fabergé *Imperial Jeweller,* exhibition catalogue, State Hermitage Museum, St Petersburg, 1993

Fresco-Corbu, Roger *Vesta Boxes,* Lutterworth Press, Cambridge, 1983

Gentle, Rupert & Field, Rachael *Domestic Metalwork, 1640–1820,* Antique Collectors' Club, Woodbridge, new ed. 1994

Gilodo, A.A. *Russian Silver – Mid 19th Century – Beginning of the 20th Century,* Beresta, Moscow, 1994

Goes, Benedict *The Intriguing Design of Tobacco Pipes,* Uniepers b.v./ Pijpenkabinet, Leiden, 1993

Helliwell, Stephen *Collecting Small Silverware,* Phaidon/ Christie's, Oxford, 1988

Hornsby, Peter *Collecting Antique Copper and Brass,* Moorland, Ashbourne, 1989

Jestin, Catherine *Powder Celestial: Snuff Boxes, 1700–1880,* Yale Center

for British Art, New Haven, Connecticut, 1990

Le Corbeiller, Clare *European and American Snuff Boxes,* Batsford, London, 1966

Le Roy, Bernard/Szafran, Maurice *The Illustrated History of Cigars,* Harold Starke Publishers, London, 1993

Mitchell, James R. *Antique Metalware,* Universe Books, New York, 1976

Rapaport, Benjamin *A Complete Guide to Collecting Antique Pipes,* Schiffer Publishing Ltd, Exton, PA, 1979

Rendell, Joan *The Match, the Box, and the Label,* David and Charles, Newton Abbot, 1983

Schneider, Stuart L. and Fischler, George *Cigarette Lighters,* Schiffer Publishing, Atglen, PA, 1996

Scott, Amoret & Christopher *Smoking Antiques,* Shire Publications Ltd, Princes Risborough, 1981 and *Tobacco and the Collector,* Max Parrish, London, 1966

Turner, Eric *An Introduction to Brass,* Victoria and Albert Museum, London, 1982

Glossary

armorial a coat of arms or crest, usually engraved on silver

Auer metal a durable amalgam of iron and cerium, creating a powerful spark when scratched; used in modern cigarette lighters

briar wood of the heath tree growing on the Mediterranean coast, widely used for pipe bowls from the mid 19thC

bright cut a form of engraving in which the surface of the metal is cut at an angle, rather than as a V-shaped groove, to reflect the light

canted flat surface made by cutting a corner at a 45 degree angle

carotte a tightly bound roll of tobacco

cloisonné type of enamel fired into small cells (*cloisons*) created by soldering metal wires onto a metal surface

die-stamping industrialized method of creating, or decorating, silver objects by pressing sheet silver between two dies with complementary patterns

electroplate metal, usually nickel or copper, plated with a thin layer of silver by using electrolysis

embossing method of creating relief decoration on metal objects by hammering, or punching, on the reverse side

enamelling decoration made by fusing a vitreous substance, usually coloured with metallic oxides, as a paste, or in an oil based medium, to metal (or ceramics or glass) under heat

engine-turning decorative, incised patterns created by turning metal on a machine-driven lathe

flat chasing method of decorating a flat metal surface by using hammers and punches to push the metal into relief

fluting decorative motif of shallow, concave, parallel, vertical grooves

fusee (also called Vesuvian or flamer) a type of match with a large head, designed for lighting a pipe or cigar out of doors

gilding decoration using gold on metal, ceramics, or glass

guilloché translucent enamel applied over a metal surface chased or engraved in low relief, often in circular or wave-like patterns

lacquer resinous substance, often applied in layers, like varnish, and used as a basis for Oriental-style decoration

lithography printing technique in which a design is drawn in ink on stone, then transferred to paper, and then to an object

malachite type of rich, copper-green stone with black veinings, found mainly in Russia

Mauchlineware wooden souvenirs, including snuff boxes, with pen and ink, painted, or printed decoration, made in Scotland from the 18thC

meerschaum opaque white/grey magnesium silicate, popular for pipe bowls in the late 19thC

mull small Scottish container for snuff, usually made from horn, and often mounted in silver

netsuke decorative, often carved, toggles used in Japan to secure a pipe case or other useful object to the sash of a kimono

niello mixture of lead, silver, copper, and sulphur, applied to an engraved or incised metal surface, and fired to create decorative, linear patterns, widely used on Russian metalwork

ormolu "gilt bronze" alloy of copper, tin, and zinc, used to imitate gold

papier-mâché moulded material made of pulped paper, glue, and chalk, often painted, or inlaid with mother of pearl, and used to make small decorative objects, such as snuff boxes

pâte-de-cristal and **pâte-de-verre** glassmaking techniques, in which glass powder is coloured with metal oxides, packed into a mould, and then fired to produce translucent, richly coloured glass, resembling hardstones

pinchbeck an alloy of copper and zinc, developed in the early 18thC as a substitute for gold

piqué work tortoiseshell inlaid with decorative patterns of gold and silver wire

shagreen finely grained sharkskin, used in Europe from the 17thC for decorating small objects such as boxes or cases

snuff powdered tobacco for inhaling through the nostrils

spelter an alloy of zinc, used as an alternative to bronze

stopper/tamper small, often carved object, with a cylindrical base, for pressing down burning tobacco in a pipe

transfer-printing method of decorating ceramics, or wood, by transferring an inked image from an engraved plate to a sheet, or a "bat", of sticky glue, and then to the object

vesta case (also called matchsafe) small, portable container for short wax matches (vestas), popular from the mid 19thC

Index

Photographic Acknowledgements

Bridgeman Art Library 13 centre, 14 centre, 15 bottom, 19 right, 23 bottom, 24 left; **Christie's Images** 1, 7 bottom, 12 top, 12 bottom, 13 top, 13 bottom, 14 left, 14 right, 15 top, 15 centre, 16 top, 16 bottom, 17 left, 17 right, 17 top, 19 centre, 22 left, 22 right, 23 right, 23 top left, 24 centre, 24 right, 25 centre, 25 right, 26 left, 26 centre, 26 right, 27 left, 27 centre, 27 right, 28 top, 30 left, 30 right, 31 top, 31 bottom, 32 top left, 32 bottom left, 33 left, 33 centre, 34 left, 36 top, 36 bottom, 37 left, 43 left, 46 top, 46 bottom, 48 centre, 55 bottom right; **Alfred Dunhill Museum and Archive/Stephen Crawley** 7 top, 8 bottom, 48 right, 49 left, 50 left, 50 right, 51 top, 51 centre, 51 bottom, 54 top, 56 top, 56 bottom, 57 bottom; **Hackney Archive** 21 right; **Octopus Publishing Group Ltd** 5, **/A. J. Photographics/Bonhams** 19 top left, **/A. J. Photographics/Christie's South Kensington** 28 bottom, **/A. J. Photographics/Fay Lucas** 34 right, 48 left, **/Steve Tanner/From the collection of Richard Ball** 57 top, 57 centre, **/Steve Tanner/Imperial War Museum** 29, 29 top, **/Steve Tanner/J. Trevor Barton Collection** 2, 4 top, 6, 8 top, 9 bottom left, 10 right, 11 top, 11 centre, 11 bottom, 18 top left, 18 right, 18 bottom, 21 left, 35 right, 35 bottom, 38 top, 39 top, 39 bottom, 40 left, 40 right, 41 top, 41 centre, 41 bottom, 42 left, 42 centre, 42 right, 43 centre, 43 right, 44 left, 44 right, 45 top, 45 centre, 47 top, 47 bottom right, **/Steve Tanner/Jacques Coles Collection** 39 centre; **Officina Alessi/Alessi Spa/Marianne Brandt** 55 bottom left, **/Alessi spa** 55 centre; **Robert Opie** 20 top, 20 bottom 37 top, 37 centre; **Phillips, London** 9 top, 9 bottom right, 31 centre, 32 right, 38 bottom, 45 right, 47 bottom left, 54 bottom, 55 top; **Ronson** 49 right, 49 centre; **Sotheby's New York** 29 left; **Photograph courtesy of Wartski, London** 33 right; **Zippo** 52 bottom, 52-53 top, 53 top, 53 bottom left, 53 bottom right

Acknowledgments

The author would like to thank Jeff Lovell at Christie's, South Kensington, Peter Tilly for advice on Alfred Dunhill Ltd, Trevor Barton for supplying numerous accessories from the J. Trevor Barton Collection, Jacques Coles for his expertise, Linda Meabon at Zippo Inc., and Jenny Faithfull and Selina Mumford at Mitchell Beazley.